Beauty *for* ASHES

DIVORCE AND THE LATTER-DAY SAINT WOMAN

C. NOELLE McBRIDE

CFI
AN IMPRINT OF CEDAR FORT, INC.
SPRINGVILLE, UTAH

This is not an official publication of The Church of Jesus Christ of Latter-day Saints. The opinions and views expressed herein belong solely to the author and do not necessarily represent the opinions or views of Cedar Fort, Inc. Permission for the use of sources, graphics, and photos is also solely the responsibility of the author.

ISBN 13: 978-1-4621-4385-6

Published by CFI, an imprint of Cedar Fort, Inc.
2373 W. 700 S., Springville, UT 84663
Distributed by Cedar Fort, Inc., www.cedarfort.com

Library of Congress Control Number: 2022938184

Cover design by Shawnda T. Craig

Printed in the United States of America

10 9 8 7 6 5 4 3 2 1

Printed on acid-free paper

To D, whose faith in me has never wavered,
and to my children—you are my greatest accomplishment.

Contents

Introduction

An Instrument in the Lord's Hands

This is not a book about how to get divorced. No one can tell you how, or even if, you should get divorced. That is a sacred decision between you and the Lord. As I embarked on this journey, I couldn't help but wish there had been a book to walk me through the process and help me understand what life would be like during and after a divorce. I did not know how to start or where to turn for direction.

This book explains my journey utilizing the saving grace of Jesus Christ's Atonement while going through a divorce. If your path and experiences look different from mine, it is not because you did anything wrong. I do not believe there is a right or wrong way to get divorced. It is an experience that unfolds minute by minute and is unique to the individuals that go through it.

As I began the path of healing, I received several gentle reminders to write my memories down. I hoped that someday I would be able to share the strength and faith I had gained through these experiences. I prayed that the Lord could use my trials to help others, that I could be an instrument in His hands.

Along the way, I realized that each of us is touched in one way or another by divorce, whether it be your own or that of a parent, family member, friend, or ward member. This compilation is designed to help the individual who is currently going through a divorce, has already experienced divorce, or desires to help a loved one navigate this particular trial.

Divorce can make you feel isolated and alone, like an outsider or a pariah. You may feel as though everything you desire for your life is utterly unattainable to you. Sometimes through divorce you lose friends, sometimes you gain friends, and sometimes you have friends re-enter your life. The adversary would have those of us experiencing divorce firsthand believe we are totally alone and that there is nothing for us in the Church.

In fact, he would have us conclude that because of our divorce, the Church or the gospel failed us entirely. We were sold a story of an eternal marriage and everlasting bliss that, in reality, only delivered continual heartache, a home torn apart, and a feeling that we do not belong anywhere. This is one of Satan's most insidious lies because if he can get you to believe you do not belong, he can separate you from the very thing that will bring you the greatest peace: the Atonement of Jesus Christ.

It is my hope that as you peruse these pages, you will find a renewed faith; that you will discover how to tap into strengths you never knew you possessed; and that these experiences will lead you to believe anew the promises our Father in Heaven has made to all His children—especially *you*.

Some of the experiences I share on these pages are sacred. Some are answers meant for me and my individual circumstances. After much thought and prayer, I have included them as a witness to the very real and tangible mercy of our Father in Heaven. My prayer is that through sharing my story, I may be an instrument in the Lord's hands, to give hope to others experiencing the same trial.

My story is one of redemption and healing, of beauty for ashes.

"God's desire that Latter-day Saints keep on trying extends beyond overcoming sin. Whether we suffer because of troubled relationships, economic challenges, or illnesses, or as a consequence of someone else's sins, the Savior's atonement can heal even- and perhaps most especially-those that have innocently suffered. He understands perfectly what it is like to have suffered innocently as a consequence of another's transgression. As prophesied the Savior will 'bind up the broken hearted, give beauty for ashes, the oil of joy for mourning, and the garment of praise for the spirit of heaviness."[1]

—Dale G. Renlund

Prologue

It is a chilly December morning. I stretch, warm and comfortable in my bed. Suddenly I am wide awake, my eyes open with excitement. It is my wedding day! At twenty years old, I have just spent my last night as a single woman in a hotel room with my parents and sisters, the Portland Temple just down the road. Eagerly I get out of bed, shower, and pull out a new makeup palette that I have specially picked out for today. I slip on my favorite dress, leave the hotel, and join the man I will soon call my husband. I am filled with confidence; I know this is exactly where I am meant to be. We are on our way to the House of the Lord.

As I enter the Portland Temple for the first time, I marvel at its beauty and majesty. At the front desk, we present our recommends and then enter the temple office. Here we sit with our parents as witnesses and sign all the requisite paperwork for the marriage. My father-in-law gently pulls me aside for a moment, and earnestly asks, "Are you sure?" I do not immediately understand his question. I then realize he is asking if I am sure I want to marry his son. I look him clearly in the eyes and state with a calm confidence, "Yes, I am sure." My declaration fills me with peace and assurance.

In the bride's room, I put on my wedding dress with the help of my mother. It is an exquisite gown designed especially for the temple. Having been previously endowed, I reverently add my temple robes. Ready now, I follow a matron who takes me to meet my groom. Catching a glimpse of myself in the hall mirror as we walk by, I am stunned at my reflection. I have never felt so beautiful. It is a kind of radiant beauty that fills every part of my being. I slowly begin to descend an enormous marble staircase. My dress sweeps gently behind me, and with each downward step, I feel like a princess. My heart is filled with so much joy; it is hard to contain.

At the bottom of the stairs, my husband-to-be is waiting. He smiles and reaches for my hand. We talk excitedly and quietly of what is to come. Together, we enter the sealing room. It is filled with family and friends. Their happiness radiates over our union. We kneel across the altar, gazing momentarily at the sparkling chandelier overhead. The officiator kindly gives us some newlywed advice. The ceremony begins.

My emotions are immediately evident to everyone in the room as happy tears run down my face. I am nervous about wiping them away, as we are in the middle of the sealing, but the sympathetic officiator pauses and encourages me to wipe my eyes. We all share a laugh, and the ceremony continues. But the joyful tears continue to return. Finally, the ceremony concludes, and we are declared husband and wife.

After stepping away from the altar, we exchange rings to much reverent fanfare from our guests. We greet them with happy and grateful hugs. We are officially married, husband and wife for time and all eternity. I have never been happier or more excited for the future.

Seventeen Years Later

I sit in a sparsely furnished room, completely alone, heart pounding, hands shaking. A stack of papers waits in front of me. Crying out a sob, I ask myself how I could possibly be at a law office, about to sign divorce papers. I recall snippets from my wedding day—a lifetime ago, now.

Then I consider the previous evening spent in the Columbia River Temple and the incredible peace I had felt regarding moving forward with this decision. Hands still trembling, I begin to sign as my tears continue. I feel the severing of my marriage with each signature. I cry aloud for the courage to continue this awful thing. I am immediately filled with a strength and peace not my own. I finish signing.

Looking down at the completed documents, I suddenly wonder if the tear stains on the pages will affect the legality of what I have signed. I gently spot-dry them and issue another silent prayer of gratitude to my Father in Heaven for the comfort I have felt. I take a deep breath, wipe the few stray tears, and step out of the room. The office is bustling with people going about their regular everyday business, completely unaware of my heavy heart. I return all the signed documents to the secretary, who smiles empathetically at my red eyes and lingering sniffles. Neither of us speaks the obvious. I walk out the door into the fading light of the autumn afternoon.

I sit for a moment in my car, futilely trying to absorb the reality of the decision I have just made. I say aloud softly, "I am divorced." The words are foreign to my ears. I realize that somewhere he will also be signing papers today. I wonder if he will cry or have the same feeling of loss as I do.

I pray once more, feeling the words in my heart and mind—a quiet recognition of the strength and courage I have been given. As I continue to sit, I feel the Spirit enter my heart with an even greater feeling of peace. It transforms the weight of my grief, and my burden is momentarily lifted.

Once again, just as I had felt on my wedding day, I know without a doubt that I am in the exact right place in my life, doing exactly what the Lord would have me do.

"It is your reaction to adversity, not the adversity itself, that determines how your life's story will develop." [1]

—Dieter F. Uchtdorf

Chapter 1

The Beginning

"You can have revelatory, profoundly instructive experiences with the Lord in the most miserable experiences of your life."[1]

—Jeffrey R. Holland

Choices

How does one go from being married—sealed for time and all eternity—to being divorced, with three children, nearly twenty years later? I do not have the answers, in all honesty. I know some issues required our bishop's help and counsel. However, there was no single thing that I could clearly point to and say, "There! That is the single reason for my divorce."

As I look back, the reasons appear to lie in a series of hundreds of small choices. Some choices were daily; some were over a period of months, others years. These little daily choices added up to decisions that then turned into habits. Those habits shaped us into the people we were seventeen years later after we were sealed for time and all eternity that chilly day in December. President Hinckley cautions, "The course of our lives is seldom determined by great, life altering decisions. Our direction is often set by the small, day to day choices that chart the track on which we run. This is the substance of our lives—making choices."[2]

There are always two parts to every divorce. My part in the story of our divorce centers around my unhealthy relationship with food. Overeating for me was a symptom of a deeper problem—a desire to escape reality. I was desperately unhappy, and it showed through unhealthy patterns of eating: bingeing, restricting, and over-exercising, all in an effort to control and limit weight gain over the years. I loved being a mother and a wife but often felt that I was falling short in my own expectations. I also felt very alone in my efforts working full-time, running a household, and trying to raise our children in a Christ-centered home. Through a series of miraculous events, I was led to a twelve-step program for my eating.

That journey began a few years before my divorce. I won a cruise to Mexico with the company I worked for. (I was an independent contractor and professional makeup artist.) The trip was "girls only," and I was excited to spend time with my coworkers/friends. It had been a year since I had seen some of them because while we worked for the same company, we all worked in different parts of the country.

My friends and I spent the first day aboard the cruise ship, exploring the various decks and talking nonstop. While exploring, I discovered food was served aboard the ship 24/7. The first night at dinner, I learned you could literally order *everything* off the menu; it was all-inclusive! I had never experienced such decadence before and thoroughly enjoyed indulging in everything food-wise.

After a couple of days on the cruise, I had a moment alone with one of the gals I was rooming with. She was fit and thin, about ten years older than me. Residing with her, I had seen her nighttime routine of Pilates and stretching exercises. I was thoroughly impressed because I was not sure I could even do a proper sit-up.

During our one-on-one conversation, she asked if I would be willing to pray for her. I was surprised and immediately replied, "Of course." I was especially touched that she asked me because we were not of the same faith. I asked, "What do you need me to pray for?"

She shared she was experiencing many severe health issues. I was shocked because she looked like she was the epitome of health. She then turned to me, cupped my cheek, and kindly said, "And I will pray for you."

I was taken aback. "What do I need any prayers for?"

She looked me straight in the eyes. "Oh, sweetie. You look so unhappy."

In that moment, my walls completely crumbled, and I cried. Someone finally had seen me, had looked past the smiles, the "everything is fine" lines, and had seen ME.

My friend and I had a good heart to heart talk. I confessed that in trying to deal with all the stress of working full-time, running the household, and all my own expectations, I had clearly been using food as a coping mechanism. I knew I needed help. After our talk, I had a spark of courage to go home and take some action.

Once home, I did some research before I lost the little determination I had gained. I decided to join a twelve-step program. I found where a local group met and attended my first meeting.

Walking in those doors for the first time was absolutely terrifying. I felt that I had reached the lowest of lows in my personal life to have to sit in that room. I listened as the other people shared and thought to myself, "Maybe I don't really have a problem. Their situations sound much worse than mine!" Before I could slip out at the end of the meeting, several members welcomed me warmly and encouraged me to keep coming back. I felt as if they could read my mind and had known I had not planned on returning.

One woman in particular encouraged me to attend six meetings before deciding anything. Although I didn't want to go back, part of me felt that attending six meetings seemed a reasonable request to prove this wasn't where I needed to be. However, after attending six meetings, I found that those meetings were precisely the place I needed to be.

After many months of attending meetings and faithfully working the program, I began to see a significant change in the way I was thinking and feeling. My relationship with my Father in Heaven grew, and I began to understand the gospel in a whole new way. I realized the expectations I'd had for myself were not my Father in Heaven's expectations.

I learned that living the gospel was not merely looking like I had everything together, but truly relying on the Lord. I had relied on myself too much. Living the steps alongside the principles of the gospel, I experienced an increase of peace in my life and felt more balanced in my roles as a mother and wife. With better balance, I slowly began to lose weight.

As a result of my weight loss, my self-confidence and self-esteem increased. I finally became willing to address some of the serious things that I felt were amiss in my marriage. Before my twelve-step program, I believed that if everything in my marriage *looked* good, then it must *be* good.

I made a list of the most pressing concerns and began to earnestly work on these issues within my marriage. Some items on my list were small adjustments that I could personally make. Other issues challenged both of us to work together as a couple and required a more long-term view of the changes that needed to be made. A year later, I was still faithfully working the twelve-step program and doing well in many areas of my life but felt discouraged at the lack of any real change for the better in my marriage. I recognized I was responsible for my choices but not anyone else's. I confided my discouragement and concerns to a good friend. After listening, my friend asked if I had sought counseling for my marriage. At that point, I had not. My friend replied with quiet intensity, "Fight. Fight for your marriage, Noelle. Fight with everything you have for your children and your home."

I realized in that moment that a part of me had given up hope that change was even possible within my home. Hearing my friend encourage me to do better for my family kindled a fire in me. The following week I met with my bishop and started counseling with a certified marriage counselor from the Church's branch of social services.

Taking Responsibility

"You must take responsibility for your own choices and actions, for you learn nothing until you take ownership of your life."[3]

—Leon Brown

Counseling enabled me to work on the things *I* could do. I had felt hopeless in the past about my ability to maintain any kind of lasting change. While working with my counselor, I learned about healthy boundaries: "Any confusion of responsibility and ownership in our lives is a problem of boundaries. . . . We need to set mental, physical, emotional, and spiritual boundaries to help us distinguish what is our responsibility and what isn't. An inability to set appropriate limits . . . can be very destructive [in our lives]."[4]

In my personal life, I struggled with the inability to say no and frequently took responsibility for things that were not my responsibility. Initially, it was difficult to realize that my choices, intentional and unintentional, concerning setting limits had made my personal life and marriage that much more difficult. I was praying daily, especially for my husband and our marriage. I asked Heavenly Father to help open my eyes so I could (1) see things accurately and (2) lovingly practice my newly learned boundaries. I also prayed to find ways that I could show my love more fully toward my husband. For an entire year, this was the plea of my heart that guided my daily thoughts and actions. I was not perfect, but the desires of my heart were good.

The Lord continued to give me the strength to make necessary small changes and to show an increase in loving behaviors toward my husband. Through regular prayer, patience, and repentance, I gained new insights on what my Heavenly Father wanted for me. As I practiced setting healthy boundaries, I felt an increase of peace that came from working to align myself with the will of my Father in Heaven.

Several months passed, and despite my prayers and months of therapy, things continued to be difficult between my husband and me. The very real issues that had come to light during counseling and with help from our bishop were not being resolved in any way. We were simply not making any progress toward any reconciliation as a couple. I felt we were not equally yoked, and our home was constantly filled with strife and anger.

I continued to work with my counselor and bishop, but I received the prompting that my spouse and I needed to separate. We had been living independently of each other within our home, but that temporary solution was no longer working. The decision to ask my husband to move out was not an easy one. I had felt the prompting to separate for months but could not bring myself to do it. I pleaded with the Lord for another way. I was terrified that separation was the answer. I honestly wondered how being apart could bring us closer together.

The Lord continued to be patient with my doubts. I went to the temple for confirmation, and I talked it over with my counselor. I wanted him to approve of my choice, to encourage me that I was doing the right thing, but he would not. In fact, he was noticeably clear in saying, "Noelle, I know you want me to say this is okay, or the right thing to do, but I can't. Only you have the right to receive that personal revelation."

Shortly after attending the temple and speaking with my counselor, events transpired within our home that made me realize that it was now imperative that I follow the whisperings of the Spirit and ask my husband to move out. In the past, when I had received similar promptings to separate, I had tried to wait and come up with the perfect plan to cause as little disruption as possible. This time, despite the fear I felt, I followed the prompting immediately.

The next morning after getting the kids out the door for school, I went for a run as my husband moved some temporary belongings out. I remember that it was a beautiful sunny morning. The sunshine was a sharp contrast to the pit of fear I felt in my stomach as I left my house. I was fearful of what long-term consequences would come from the decision to separate. I did not know what was next for our little family. But, as I ran, a feeling of peace descended over me. I realized I had grown in strength and faith to such a degree that being obedient to the Spirit was more important to me than anything else. This realization was of great comfort.

As I returned home and entered my house an hour later, there was a different feel to the entire space. As I looked around, it seemed brighter and lighter. Suddenly, I was filled with the Holy Ghost to a fulness I had not been able to feel in my own home for so long. I sat on my couch and wept. I thanked my Heavenly Father for the courage to do what I had thought was impossible.

Several days passed after our separation, during which time I met with my bishop and counselor. We worked together to set a plan to help me feel as though I were moving forward despite the reality that I was in a holding pattern with my husband. I was still hopeful that our time apart would allow us to work through our issues and eventually reunite.

My counselor and I made a simple list of changes that would need to occur during our time apart to help us determine if our separation had achieved its desired purpose. Within a few short weeks, it became apparent that the changes were not happening. In frustration, I began to pray for understanding about what the next step should be. Again, the Spirit reminded me that I could not control anyone else's choices but my own. Changing my prayers to focus on *my* next steps helped me have more patience and trust the Lord's timing. Elder Uchtdorf's words gently reminded me to continue to have faith when he stated, "We cannot force God to comply with our desires—no matter how right we think we are or how sincerely we pray."[5]

During the separation, I spent a lot of time in prayer and reflecting on my life. I realized that many of my best attributes, such as being strong-willed and determined, had been frequently viewed by those closest to me as negative qualities. To compensate, I tried minimizing myself as much as possible. I put all my wants and needs on the back burner, tending to everyone's needs first.

Through counseling and my twelve-step work, I realized that the negative perceptions of my attributes were not negative at all. My attributes were really gifts from a loving Heavenly Father. But the years of thinking and hearing the worst concerning my talents and gifts had led me to doubt my self-worth. Due to my current calling in the Young Women organization and my struggle with self-confidence, my counselor suggested that I complete the Young Women Personal Progress program again. I loved the idea! Plus, it gave me something solid to focus on while I was waiting.

As I began reading the Personal Progress booklet's inspired words, my mind was flooded with thoughts and feelings I had not considered in years. I felt as if I had forgotten all the lessons I had learned as a youth when I had completed the Personal Progress program the first time and earned my Young Women medallion. I realized that survival mode had been my normal for many years. This new program was slightly different than the one I had completed, but the essentials were the same. Slowly, my mindset toward myself began to shift.

My self-worth became less contingent on what other people thought or felt about me and more focused on what my Father in Heaven felt and thought about me. What He wanted for my children and I became of paramount importance. Working on the Personal Progress program was a sacred experience for me. It reminded me of who I was and what my Heavenly Father needed me to do in this life. Focusing my energies in this direction strengthened my ability to listen more intently to others' needs, especially those of my children. Recognizing and honoring my own needs also became easier. As a result, an even greater balance developed within our family and home.

After several months, the changes my counselor and I had discussed would need to happen for my husband's and my separation to end still had not occurred. In fact, there were several more issues that came to light during this time that led me to believe that any kind of reconciliation would be impossible. I prayed fervently to know what I should do next.

As I prayed and studied the scriptures, I felt the overall impression I needed to ask for a divorce. The idea was awful to me—devastating on every level. Yet, when I tried other courses of action, my way became blocked every time. I prayed for weeks to know if I should move ahead with a divorce but did not receive a clear answer in my mind. At that point, I was simply asking the Lord if I should get divorced or not. When I spoke to my counselor, he suggested that instead of asking a question, I make a decision and then pray to know if I should move forward with that decision.

Receiving Revelation

"Personal revelation is a powerful, persuasive antidote to uncertainty and confusion."[6]

—Sheri Dew

With my counselor's advice in mind, I made the choice to remain married. I told the Lord I was willing to do whatever was required. I had invested everything in our marriage. We had seventeen years of history and three boys who were my world.

With that decision made, I went to the temple for additional insight on what to do next. As I sat in the temple that day, I felt as though the heavens were closed. I received no confirmation that my decision was right. I felt uneasy and anxious. Later that night, when I returned home, I knelt and prayed. I felt nothing and heard only silence. I retired to bed but could not sleep. I lay awake and thought about the silence from the Holy Ghost I was experiencing. It was a stark contrast to the constant stream of inspiration I had previously felt and had come to expect over the past year.

As I continued to lie in bed and begin to drift off, certain phrases in my patriarchal blessing kept coming to my mind. I had been studying my blessing as part of my journey through the Personal Progress program, and I had noticed that several key promises had yet to be fulfilled in any measure. While I was half-asleep and pondering, my mind was illuminated, and I understood that if I chose to stay on my current path, those blessings the Lord had in store for me could not be fulfilled. I clearly saw two paths before me: one was flooded with a bright light; everything was lush and green. The other path was lifeless, dark, and desolate.

I fell asleep, pondering these thoughts. When I awoke in the morning, I still recalled the powerful dream-like scene I had witnessed. After more thought, I got on my knees, trembling, and told the Lord what I remembered of the two paths. I spoke out loud. I said that I would choose the path He would have for me, not what I wanted. With tears streaming down my face, I told Him that I felt that I needed to get a divorce. My whole being, though shaking with this decision, was instantly filled with peace and light, and I felt a confirmation that divorce was the path I must take.

After determining my course, I waited a couple of days before moving forward with any action. I wanted to ponder the message I had received from the Holy Ghost. Frequently when I thought of what my course was really going to mean, I felt paralyzed by the "hows" and "whys." Then, I would burst into tears, feeling as though my heart was breaking in half.

Each time I felt completely overwhelmed, I would turn to the Lord in prayer. Every time I asked for a confirmation, I felt comfort and peace. After a week, I decided to go to the temple before moving forward with actually filing for divorce. By this point, I had told my mom and sister of my plans. My sister was not surprised that I had decided to file for divorce. She and her husband had observed several alarming issues throughout the years, and she had been actively praying that I would be able to confide in her when I was ready. My mom had a different reaction. She encouraged me to find a way to "work it out." She just could not believe that divorce was the answer. Hearing her doubts began to work on my mind. I was terrified of making the wrong choice, terrified of the long-term effects this would have on my children and my eternal family.

Burgeoning Peace

"Because of His pain, in the midst of ours, we can find peace."[7]

—Laurel C. Day

In retrospect, I believe that the Lord understood the magnitude of faith that I would need in order to get through a trial of this degree. As a result, He willingly poured out His Spirit upon me. He patiently held my hand through the whole process and blessed me with peace each time I stumbled or wavered in my faith.

One such precious moment came one day just prior to attending the temple. I sat in my room, pondering the scriptures I was reading and writing in my journal. I wrote down my fears of making the wrong decision for my family. Afterward I read these words in the scriptures: "Be strong and of good courage, fear not, nor be afraid for them: for the Lord thy God, he that is doth go with thee; he will not fail thee, nor forsake thee."[8]

I felt prompted to look at my patriarchal blessing again. As I read the sacred words of my blessing, a phrase seemed to leap off the page. In my blessing, I was told that I would make the right choices if I counseled with the Lord and made each decision in my life prayerfully. Knowing that I had done just that alleviated my fears and allowed me to move forward with more confidence.

My next step was to go to the temple to receive confirmation of the promptings I had received. I asked my family to fast and pray for me. In response, and to show her support, my mom offered to attend the temple with me. I was grateful to have her company.

My heart was full while we attended the endowment session together. Afterward, I sat in the celestial room, taking in the beauty and incomparable peace found only in that holy space. My mother had entered the room before me and sat in her own contemplative prayer. I took advantage of the relative privacy of the moment by seeking out a quiet spot to pray and ponder as well.

I had come to the Lord's holy house that day to seek a confirmation that my decision to move forward with divorcing my husband was the correct one. As I pondered the decisions before me, I walked to a table to get a set of scriptures and then returned to my seat. I prayed quietly in my heart as I paged through the Book of Mormon. I turned to my favorite book, Jacob. Not knowing what I was looking for, I began reading Jacob 5, the parable of the olive tree. I skimmed through most of the verses but began to read in earnest around verses 41–46. When I got to verse 47, I had a hard time not gasping aloud. The verses I read mirrored what I had been asking the Lord: "Tell me what more I need to do." Verse 47 answered:

> But what could I have done more for my vineyard. Have I slackened mine hand, that I have not nourished it? Nay, I have nourished it, and I have digged about it, and I have pruned it, and I have dunged it; and I have stretched forth mine hand almost all the day long, and the end draweth nigh. And it grieveth me that I should hew down all the trees in my vineyard and cast them into the fire that they should be burned. Who is it that has corrupted my vineyard?[8]

As I sat in the celestial room, I knew without a shadow of a doubt that I had done all that the Lord required of me to save my marriage. I had "nourished it," I had "dug about and pruned it."

My time of waiting through our separation had been analogous to "my hand outstretched still," and I was "grieving the loss of this tree." My whole being was filled with such peace. Tears streamed down my face. I knew this scripture was the answer to my prayer.

That moment in the temple was nothing short of a small miracle for me.

As I finished reading and said a prayer of gratitude for the sweet experience I'd had, my mom joined me. Her face was filled with light. She gently grasped my arm in a half embrace and whispered to me, "Noelle, I don't know how, but I know everything is going to be all right, and that you are being led by the Spirit." Even with the passage of time, the deep conviction of the truthfulness of my mother's words is still written on my soul. I count that experience in the temple as one of the most sacred witnesses in my life. Indeed, as Elder Neil L. Andersen has said, "The peace of the temple [was] a soothing balm to [my] wounded soul."[9]

Despite the reassurances from my Heavenly Father that I was on the right path, it was difficult and heartbreaking to begin to move forward with the steps of getting a divorce. I had no knowledge of the process and felt I needed legal advice. I asked a good friend for the name of a lawyer. She suggested Mr. Smith, a lawyer who practiced locally. I went to my first meeting, armed with a list of questions, and my mother joined me again for support. Mr. Smith answered all my questions and gave me a plethora of other information.

The most shocking fact I learned was that the state in which we lived had a ninety-day waiting period—a time designated to allow things to "cool off" (in case either party changed their mind). Once you filed the paperwork for the divorce, the ninety days began. After all my praying and fasting, waiting and agonizing over my decision, I just wanted to move forward with my life. Hearing that yes, we could begin the process, but no, not yet was very difficult, especially when the waiting period was an additional ninety days!

After the divorce paperwork was officially filed, I sent a letter notifying my husband of my intention. I had wrestled mentally about whether to have a face-to-face conversation with him or to write a letter. Ultimately, I decided that in light of my emotions, I could express my thoughts more coherently in a letter. I prayed for direction and took a few days to write the letter. I then signed to have it delivered with the divorce papers.

When I next met with my bishop, I informed him that (1) I had already begun the process of filing for divorce and that (2) I had sent a letter to my husband telling him of my intent. The letter explained that I was acting in accordance with what I felt were the Lord's desires for us. The bishop was kind and sympathetic as he listened, but then he asked me if I would wait. I was so confused. I could not understand why he was asking me to wait. He explained that he felt prompted to ask me to wait before taking any more action with the divorce proceedings.

I cannot express the internal struggle I felt in that moment. I knew I had received my answer from my Heavenly Father, but I also knew the bishop had been called of God. Moments passed while I mentally struggled with how to reply to his request. I felt that his appeal that I wait to move forward with any more action was in direct conflict with the answer I had received to proceed with the divorce. I silently prayed for guidance.

Soon I felt a calm settle over me. The bishop's request did not make sense to me, but with the comfort of the Spirit, I could agree to what he asked. I would wait. I would not move forward yet with any further legal proceedings. I found comfort in Paul Alan Cox's words, "We must not despair because the Lord's timetable is different from ours, sometimes we just have to wait."[10]

Through a series of phone calls over the next few days, my husband replied to my letter and the divorce papers. The conversations were consistently heated and produced no progress toward reconciliation. After a week had passed, he told me that he had attended the temple the night before and wanted to share an experience with me. I agreed to have a conversation about it. As I prepared to hear his experience, I became cautiously hopeful. I thought that maybe this was the reason why the bishop asked me to wait. Maybe this conversation would be the turning point for us, and we could still reconcile.

We met. My husband related to me that he had attended a temple session, during which he had felt impressed that he should not get divorced. I was surprised by the direction of the conversation. His answer was in direct conflict with the numerous impressions I had already received. I honestly did not know what to say. I remember sharing some of my thoughts with him about why I felt the way I did. He kept repeating that he had received the direction to not get divorced. I considered his words, then recommended that we both pray about our answers and move forward after concentrated prayer.

I went home and immediately got on my knees. I was so frustrated and upset by the whole conversation. I felt that the answer I had received had been reinforced several times. But, if so, then why did the bishop ask me to wait? And how could my husband have been led in a completely different direction? Nothing made sense to me anymore. I was angry with the Lord. It had taken an immense amount of faith to begin this process. Now it seemed that there were differing answers left and right. In the moment I doubted the words in the scriptures, "Know ye not that ye are in the hands of God?"[11]

That night, I returned home and tucked each of my children in bed, temporarily setting aside the distress I was feeling. After the house was quiet, I knelt at my bed and prayed for understanding. As I cried out to the Lord in my confusion and despair, I felt the peaceful calm of the Spirit come over me. My mind quieted. Finally, I found myself willing to listen to what the Lord was saying in reply to my petition. Very clearly, an answer came to my mind that my husband had indeed received the answer that he was not supposed to get divorced. That was the answer *he* had been given. It was not my answer, but *his.* How he chose to act on it would be up to him.

I felt a huge weight lift off me. I realized I had not gotten the wrong answer, and he had gotten the right one. We had each been given our own answers, and we each had our agency to choose how we would act on those. Further, our bishop (under inspired guidance) had asked me to wait. I now saw that I was to wait and see what my husband chose to do with the answer he had received. The Spirit confirmed the answer I received with peace in my heart.

With this understanding, I confidently followed the counsel of my bishop. I waited. I did not file any more legal paperwork and continued to attend my counseling sessions. After an additional three months, it was plain to see that no issues were being resolved between my husband and me due to circumstances not in my control. I knew that it was time to move forward with the divorce. I met with my bishop again and informed him of my intention. He was supportive of my decision to now move forward. He thanked me for my willingness to follow his counsel faithfully. Ninety days later, following negotiations regarding our household items and our parenting plan, we were officially divorced.

"At times . . . we feel surrounded by the pain of broken hearts, the disappointment of shattered dreams, and the despair of vanished hopes . . . We feel abandoned, heartbroken, alone. If you find yourself in such a situation, I plead with you to turn your Heavenly Father in faith. He will lift you and guide you. He will not always take your afflictions from you, but He will comfort and lead you with love through whatever storm you face." [12]

—Thomas S. Monson

Lessons Learned: Chapter 1

1. There is no right or wrong way to get divorced. This decision is between you and the Lord.
2. Invest in counseling.
3. Take responsibility for your part of the story. Divorces do not occur alone; it takes two to tango.
4. You cannot control anyone else's choices but your own.
5. Seek the Lord's approval for your decisions, value His opinion above all others.
6. Be willing to wait on the Lord. Sometimes it takes time to understand what the next step is. Trust in the Lord's timing. It is always perfect.
7. Work on a personal self-improvement course (the new "strive to be" on churchofjesuschrist.org is a great resource.)
8. Instead of asking a question and expecting an answer, make a decision and pray for confirmation.
9. Read your patriarchal blessing often (or get one, if you don't have yours yet).
10. Consider where you are going for answers. Ask yourself if they are trustworthy sources (scriptures, prayer, blessings, temple, trusted leaders, and family).

Our ability to worthily receive divine revelation is contingent on our willingness to act on the knowledge we receive. That is what I believe Moroni meant when he referred to as real intent: "And when ye shall receive these things, I would exhort you that ye would ask God, the Eternal Father, in the name of Christ, if these things are not true; and if ye shall ask with a sincere heart with real intent, having faith in Christ, he will manifest the truth of it unto you, by the power of the Holy Ghost. And by the power of the Holy Ghost ye may know the truth of all things."[13] The Lord knows the intent of our hearts and whether we are willing to obey what He tells us to do.

Chapter 2
Joy Amid Sorrow

"Shadows of despair are dispelled by rays of hope, sorrow yields to joy, and the feeling of being lost . . . vanishes with the certain knowledge that our Heavenly Father is mindful of each of us." [1]

—Thomas S. Monson

Tender Mercies

With the divorce papers signed and having received primary custody of my children, I was eager to move forward to a new chapter in my life. However, within a week, I felt a deep sadness despite my sure testimony that I was doing the right thing. I mourned the loss of our family unit, the picture in my head of the happy life I had wanted for my children and myself.

I struggled to adjust to this new normal and all the emotions it entailed. When my sons visited their father, I missed them deeply and found myself at loose ends, not knowing what to do with myself or my time. At the same time, I would feel guilty for the relief it was to have a break from the demands of being a single parent full-time.

I realized that there would be many emotions and challenges I would have to work through before moving forward to a happier chapter of my life. One of the most immediate challenges was finding a new home. As part of our divorce provision, my ex-husband received the house we had lived in for ten years. I needed to find a rental home for myself and my children. I also knew I would need help packing and moving from our current house.

Up until this point, I had limited telling anyone beyond immediate family members of my divorce. I began to fast and pray for inspiration about telling people discreetly but in a way that would enable us to receive the support needed, especially from our ward family. I felt that if there was even *one* person in our ward, I could tell without fear of judgment, that would make things a little easier. I didn't know it yet, but I was about to see a fulfillment of Sister Reyna Aburto's promise, "Miracles happen when the children of God work together, guided by the Spirit to reach out to others in need."[2]

Rose, an acquaintance from my ward, unexpectedly called to make an appointment for me to give her a facial and makeover while I was preparing to move and looking for a rental home. She and I had a wonderful time visiting and catching up on what was happening with each of our children. As we talked, I kept feeling like she was prolonging the visit. I felt as if she had something more on her mind other than the lightweight subjects we were discussing. Suddenly she paused, took a breath, and blurted out all in one rush, "Noelle, I didn't just come for an appointment with you today. I had a prompting to reach out specifically to you. Is everything okay?"

I sat back in my chair for a moment, absorbing what she had just asked. Part of me wondered if she had heard something about my circumstances, but as I listened to the Spirit to try and discern her intent, I felt only peace. I realized she was a direct answer to my prayers. That morning I had prayed very specifically, "Lord, how do I let other people in our ward know?" With Rose's inquiry, I knew the Lord had answered my prayer. I felt peace as the Spirit confirmed that it was all right to confide my circumstances to her. She was not judgmental. She kept my confidences.

She immediately got to work, helping us find a rental home and assisted in packing up our current house. Later on, she helped me get on new insurance, aided me with my job, and many more things. Her friendship was a great comfort to me as I adjusted to being a single mom. She prayed and fasted for my little family and gently ministered to us, in small and large ways. I am eternally grateful she listened to the Spirit prompting her to call me that day. Rose epitomized Sheri Dew's words, "Do we not realize the power we have to bless and heal and soothe and urge each other onward?"[3]

My sister was another angel who ministered in particular ways to our family during this time. When I called, she listened. When I was tired, she encouraged me to keep putting one foot in front of the other. She also helped with packing up items from our family home. One day, she showed up, complete with empty boxes to fill, ready to help. I had planned to begin by tackling the kitchen with her.

However, when she arrived, she told me that she felt prompted to help me take down and pack all our family pictures and memorabilia. That was the last thing I wanted to do! Although I had made the decision for our divorce, in my heart of hearts, I did not want to face the fact that our little family was changing forever.

My sister seemed to instinctively understand. She took my arm and walked with me from room to room. Together we took down all the pictures and tender reminders of my married life. I had no idea how difficult that process would be for me. I cried and cried while we packed away family portraits, baby images, and wedding mementos.

Each picture and item we bundled up felt as though I was losing my little family unit all over again. I was so grateful that my sister was there for me through that overwhelming task. Somehow she understood I could not have done it alone. Henry B. Eyring taught, "Most people carrying heavy loads begin to doubt themselves and their own worth. We lighten their loads as we are patient with their weaknesses and celebrate whatever goodness we can see in them. The Lord does that."[4] My sister's quiet act of service lightened my load and helped me take another important step toward accepting my new reality.

Another woman who served our family in an exceptional way was my Relief Society president. Shortly after I had told the bishop of my intention to get a divorce, she appeared at my doorstep. There was no call ahead of time. She just came. When she knocked, I opened the door, and before I could say anything other than hello, she said, "Noelle, the bishop has let me know you are getting a divorce. I don't know any of the details, and I don't ever need to know them. I just wanted to say I'm sorry, and I know this must be the hardest thing you've ever had to experience."

Tears immediately came to my eyes. I reached out and held her hand, trying to hold back the sobs welling up in my throat. I was still dreading future attempts to explain my decision to other people, especially my ward family. My Relief Society president's next words calmed my troubled heart. "I will let all the necessary people know, so you will hopefully be able to avoid anyone asking you questions. You don't have to say or explain anything to anyone."

I hugged that good woman! Then, I thanked her for her unconditional love and her willingness to help make this difficult transition as smooth as possible. Her visit that day was another direct answer to my prayers and a tender mercy from my Heavenly Father.

Years later, I realized that my Relief Society president had informed people so discreetly that some ward members did not even know of my divorce until well after I had moved out of the area. My Relief Society president exemplified Cheryl Esplin's teachings, "We give service when we don't criticize, refuse to gossip, stop judging, smile, say thank you, and are patient and kind."[5] My Relief Society president's compassion and sensitivity were inspiring. She was indeed on the Lord's errand.

Another blessing came when we finally found a rental home. The homeowner was a past member from our ward and could have rented it for more money, but he generously agreed on a reduced amount that allowed me to pay my rent, get on my feet financially, and provide for my children. Being self-employed, I could not always rely on a predictable amount of monthly income. The rental house was well-maintained and spacious, and it gave my children the much-needed stability of remaining in the same ward. As a bonus, its location was in a neighborhood near some of our good friends.

While we lived in that rental home, we saw the fulfillment of President Kimball's words: "God does notice and watches over us, but it is usually through another person that he meets our needs. Therefore, it is vital that we serve one another in the kingdom. So often our acts of service consist of simple encouragement or of giving mundane help with mundane tasks, but what glorious consequences can flow from mundane acts and from small but deliberate deeds!"[6] We had a host of brothers and sisters who regularly made sure we were well-taken care of while adjusting to our new life. These saints lovingly served our family by mowing our lawn, raking leaves, or shoveling snow from the driveway. All of our needs were met!

A month after moving into our rental home, the Christmas season arrived. In years past, my former spouse and I frequently relied on the Church for financial assistance during the holidays. Being self-sufficient while single had motivated me to make some financial sacrifices early on once our separation was final so I could independently provide a good holiday for my children. That season the house was festively decorated, the tree lit and trimmed with ornaments, and ten days before Christmas, I had everything purchased and wrapped for my sons. The presents under the tree were simpler this year, but I felt immense pride that I was not dependent on anyone else's generosity for the first time in several years.

Christmas Eve night, there was a loud knock on our front door. I had just finished tucking my children into bed after one of our favorite holiday traditions, reading a different Christmas themed story each night. But the knock was loud enough that all three boys sat up in bed wide-eyed. My eight-year-old asked if it was Santa at the door. I smiled at his child-like enthusiasm and told my boys to wait right there in their beds. I walked down the hall to the front door and looked outside. I could not see anyone on the front porch but instead noticed a large black bag sitting on the welcome mat.

Not sure what I was looking at, I cautiously opened the door and peeked inside the bag. I found three very nice gifts, especially picked with each of my sons in mind. Tears came to my eyes, realizing that someone had "Secret Santa-ed" our family. I discreetly brought the bag inside and finished tucking my children in their beds, reminding them that Santa could not come until they were fast asleep.

After my boys fell asleep, I pulled out each of the gifts and marveled at the kindness and generosity of whoever had purchased them for my sons. I then wrapped and labeled each of the presents and placed them under our tree. When I was finished, I sat on the couch and enjoyed the peace and magic of the holiday. I thought of the gift and miracle of the Savior's birth. I whispered a quiet prayer of gratitude to my Father in Heaven, my heart full as I reflected on our own little Christmas miracle that season.

A few weeks later, as Valentine's Day approached, I was dreading the holiday of "love" in my first year as a divorced woman. When the day arrived, so did many loving texts from friends and family, plus two dozen roses from my thoughtful dad. The accompanying card from him and my mother reminded me that I never wanted to settle for less than the eternal love I saw mirrored in their marriage. The gestures from so many made me realize there was more than just "couple love" to celebrate on Valentine's Day. There was happiness and joy to be found in relationships with friends and family.

The day after I received those beautiful flowers and messages, my former husband called me and informed me that he wanted a temple divorce because he was newly engaged. At the time of our divorce, I did not feel the need to file for an official sealing cancellation. I firmly believed that there was power in that sealing. I knew that as I chose to keep my covenants and obey the Lord, He, in turn, would bless my sons and me more fully. However, this news made me wonder how a temple divorce would affect my sealing to my children.

I met with my bishop to learn the process for the dissolution of a temple marriage. He explained that each former spouse is required to privately fill out paperwork detailing their marriage and reasons for their subsequent divorce. Then the presiding bishop for each spouse would read the completed paperwork and decide the necessary next step, either to send it onto the stake president or continue to counsel with the members seeking the cancellation. If the bishop forwarded it to the stake president for consideration, it could then be sent to the First Presidency. Neither spouse would read what the other wrote. Throughout the entire process, it was up to the bishop and stake president's discretion and inspiration as to whether the request was sent for consideration to the First Presidency.

The 2020 Church handbook clarifies this further, stating: "Members who are divorced but still sealed to the former spouse are often troubled by the sealing. The sealing will not be compulsory in the post-mortal life for either man or a woman. If temple covenants are broken, and no repentance is made, the sealing between husband and wife is revoked. However, those who keep their covenants will retain individual blessings provided by the sealing. This is the case even if the spouse has broken the covenants or withdrawn from the marriage."[7]

I felt such relief knowing those blessings were mine, regardless of other's actions. With peace in my heart, I filled out my portion of the form and turned it into our bishop. Elder Bednar's words were especially reassuring during this time: "The Lord's tender mercies are very personal, individualized blessings, strength, protection, assurances, guidance, loving-kindness, consolation, support and spiritual gifts that we receive from because of and through the Lord, Jesus Christ."[8] While I felt a mild twinge of sorrow over this last and final severing of my marriage, I recognized the Lord's many tender mercies in my life, and I did not object to either my spouse or I moving forward with our lives.

Another considerable adjustment that first year lay in navigating church. I appreciated that leaders continued to be mindful of me and the needs of my family. I had great ministering sisters and brothers assigned to our family that happily looked for ways to serve us. Each week my ministering sister, Carol, made sure to sit with me in Relief Society and Sunday School.

However, the hardest acclimation of all was the Sundays I would go from having my sons sit with me to sitting alone in an empty pew, the Sundays when the boys sat with their dad. And, yes, my ex and I continued to be in the same ward (which was excruciating)! The Lucas and Franklin families assigned themselves to look for me, specifically on the weeks my sons were with their dad, making certain I never had to sit alone. Other friends, Mary or Linda, would find me immediately after sacrament meeting and walk with me to my classes, ensuring that I was never caught unaware in awkward conversations in the hall.

Through all these adjustments, I continued to experience progress in my life. I met with my counselor weekly, and just two months after my divorce became final, I finished earning the Young Women Personal Progress medallion. Earning my medallion felt like an amazing accomplishment amid everything else going on. The bishop presented my medallion to me in front of the ward. He bore his testimony that he had personally seen me striving to draw closer to my Heavenly Father, and he noted my growing testimony of the healing power of Christ's Atonement in my own life.

It felt good to stand in front of my ward family that day—just a short time after my divorce with that kind of support. Despite best intentions from ward members, I had felt very conspicuous at church, as if I had an arrow that said "DIVORCED" pointed at my head. Ward members did not openly ask me questions, and everyone was kind and supportive, yet I felt as though my very private life had been made very public. I assumed that people had many unanswered questions. Still, I continued to be confident that I did not need to answer anyone's questions or explain anything about my situation unless I was certain it would help our situation.

As I mentioned before, my ex-husband moved back into our old home. After my sons and I moved into our rental house, their father and I continued to be in the same ward. Being in the same ward with my former spouse was awkward and led to more than a few uncomfortable situations for both of us. It became particularly unbearable when his fiancée consistently began to join him for church. It only took a few times of attending church with both of them before I made arrangements to attend my parents' ward indefinitely. There was one incident in particular that pushed me to make that decision immediately.

I awoke early one Sunday morning, determined to be on time, but despite my best efforts, we were running a little late. We walked into the chapel during the opening hymn. I looked around for a place to sit, hoping to avoid being anywhere in the vicinity of my former spouse. I did not see him in his usual spot and relaxed my guard. I spied an open pew close to the front of the chapel.

I quickly clasped my sons' hands and directed them toward the empty pew. As we walked front and center toward the open space, I suddenly realized that the very people I was trying to discreetly avoid were occupying the other half of the pew we were about to sit in. I was mortified. I frantically looked around for another open space. Anywhere else! Thankfully, another family quickly made room for my sons and me, but it took the rest of the opening hymn and prayer for my heart to stop pounding.

That same day I told my bishop that I would be attending my parents' ward from now on (which was thankfully in the same stake). I needed church to be a place where I could relax and concentrate on feeling the Spirit. Being in the chapel each week with my former spouse and his fiancée was too stressful for me. I always felt like I had to be on guard. Plus, I was still dealing with the emotional truth that we had been husband and wife just a couple of months ago. There were moments when I would see my ex from a distance, and my heart would leap treacherously in recognition of him. Logically, I knew we were not married and that I had been the one to ask for the divorce, but I was experiencing emotional whiplash at how quickly everything had changed.

I spoke to my counselor concerning these thoughts and reactions. He had a simple answer: "Noelle, it sounds as though you are still in love with him." I was shocked and embarrassed! Hearing I was still in love with my ex-husband was the last thing I had expected. I was sure that something must be wrong with me to continue to have feelings for this man, especially when he was engaged to someone else, but my counselor assured me that my feelings were normal and made perfect sense.

I had spent almost two decades with this man. I had invested my heart and soul into making our marriage work and creating a family with him. Just because we now had a piece of paper proving that we were no longer married did not mean that I had suddenly stopped loving him. My counselor encouraged me to be patient with myself and realize that it would take time for my heart to catch up with what I understood logically in my head. During this time, I relied on Elder Uchtdorf's promise, "Please understand that what you see and experience now is not what forever will be. You will not feel loneliness, sorrow, pain, and discouragement forever. We have the faithful promise of God that he will neither forget nor forsake those who incline their hearts to Him."[9]

Around this time, my sister encouraged me to go to a doctor and ask about the potential benefits of antidepressants. I was still struggling with discouragement daily and frequently called my sister crying over every frustration or difficulty. At first, I was against the idea of antidepressants. I was determined to "will" myself out of the grief I felt over the loss of my marriage. But after a few more weeks, I realized I wasn't able to "will" myself out of my emotions, so I scheduled an appointment with a local doctor. After listening to my situation and concerns, the doctor prescribed a mild antidepressant, along with a follow-up appointment.

Within a month, I began to feel more like myself. Slowly but surely, I found a better emotional balance and more things to be happy about. I chose to stay on my antidepressants for several months. The medication was simply one more tool I could use to help me combat the discouragement my circumstances had caused, and help me move forward with hope.

Through counseling, I learned that grief and healing are different for every person. There is no one formula. Most reputable books or articles about grief usually list five stages: denial, anger, bargaining, depression, and acceptance. However, there is no set order for these feelings. You do not pass through each stage of grief into the next until you finally finish and find yourself done with grieving.

Grief is frequently associated with the death of a loved one. A divorce is very much like a death. Just like in the loss of a loved one, there is an enormous sense of sorrow for what could have been and what is missing in your life. Acknowledging my grief and being proactive with my self-care helped me not fall into the trap of rushing the healing process.

Dating Again?

"May God bless the woman deep within me, the woman I'm trying to be. May He mend where my heart is broken and fill every empty space. May He erase the fears of my past to create in me a brighter future. May He make me slow to anger and quick to forgive. Amen."[10]

—Author Unknown

In an effort to embrace my new life as a single woman, a few of my friends tried to set me up on some dates. But the thought of jumping back into the dating game was terrifying to me on many levels. I knew I did not want to get into a relationship until I understood what had gone wrong in my previous one. I was afraid of making the same mistakes. I needed to pause and catch my breath. It had only been a short time since my divorce.

I did not know what to say when my friends, Lucy or Jackie, approached me with the idea of going on a date. I did say "no" emphatically, although I knew my "no's" in the past had been frequently mistaken for shyness or a demure reluctance on my part. Everyone I knew who had been divorced seemed to follow the pattern of immediately plunging into the online dating pool. But I felt as though I did not even have my head above water with the whole "single mom thing," so how could I even contemplate bringing anyone else into that? Not to mention the possible long-term effects dating again could have on my children!

When I told my counselor my feelings about dating, he supported my desire to wait before dating again. He suggested I serve a mission instead. I laughed right out loud. How was I supposed to serve a mission with three children and a full-time job? He explained that I could live like a sister missionary in that I would not date or subscribe to online dating sites for an extended period of months. I would have a specific time set aside each day for scripture study and prayer. I could continue to serve others, work full-time, and grow my personal relationship with my Savior while caring for my children.

My initial reaction? That's impossible! However, when I pondered President Nelson's words, "When the Savior knows that you truly want to reach up to him—when He can feel that the greatest desire of your heart is to draw His power into your life—you will be led by the Holy Ghost to know exactly what you should do."[11] Then, as I really considered and prayed about the idea, I loved it. And I did it! "Serving a mission" also gave me the perfect reply to well-meaning friends wanting to set me up. I recognized that this plan was a bit unconventional and maybe not the solution for everyone. But for me, serving a mission in this way gave me a fresh focus and daily purpose.

I began to read and study my scriptures with a renewed fervor. I spent even more time on my knees, talking to my Heavenly Father.

I felt relieved to be fully present with my children and their needs. I had so much fun planning what we could do together as a family. These things were never huge, nor did they cost a lot of money. They were about spending time together and making memories. We had homemade pizza parties and movie nights, went swimming with neighbors, visited family members, and took long walks on trails while picking raspberries and blackberries. We took even longer road trips. We spent time with good friends, going to the zoo, visiting beautiful landmarks, roller skating, building forts, and having Nerf gunfights. I loved watching my children laugh. I came to realize that we were still a family, even though things were different.

During this time, sister missionaries were assigned to serve in the ward I was attending. Having the sisters in the ward seemed like another way the Lord was letting me know He was personally aware of me. I grew very close to these young women and went on splits with them whenever I was available. I taught them how to do their hair and makeup and how to cook. I gave them lots of simple tips and tricks to running a household. I was available whenever they needed a ride. I tried to be a good friend to each of them. Seeing their happy, smiling faces as they served the Lord each day lifted my spirits and made me more determined to find joy in this new life I was creating.

Another plus to "serving a mission" was that it gave me time. I used this time to reflect and learn new patterns and tools to someday move forward with a healthier and happier relationship. I must say that at this point in my life, I did not believe the kind of man I wanted existed. (I had become a little bit cynical.) I joked that he was probably already married if he were to exist, and frankly, that was a problem. To help my heart from becoming too closed, my counselor gave me the assignment to write a list or letter of what I would want in a partner if I ever chose to remarry or even date again.

It took a few weeks, but I took my counselor's suggestion to heart and wrote my own version of a "Mr. Darcy list." (Mr. Darcy is a character in Jane Austen's novel *Pride and Prejudice*. He is often considered a "Prince Charming," of sorts. Avid readers of Austen might disagree with that simple description of Darcy.) One anonymous writer explained that "finding Mr. Darcy is finding an intellectual partner and equal who understands you and will mature with you." I love that explanation of Darcy best! It describes what I hoped for in a future husband.

My actual list was very purposeful. It touched on specific areas my counselor and I had discussed that were important to me. It also included aspects of what I hoped a healthy future relationship would look like.

Five Qualities I want in my future husband:

1. Loves God, above all else. Reaches and strives to fulfill and keep his covenants. He will show this by:
   - having a strong testimony
   - reading his personal scriptures
   - holding couple's prayers
   - participating in family scripture study
   - attending the temple and asking me to go with him
   - keeping his temple covenants and wanting me to keep them as well
   - keeping the Sabbath day holy
   - instigating family home evening/Come Follow Me
   - serving others
   - being trustworthy
2. Must adore and love me. He will show this by:
   - leaving me love notes and letters
   - wanting to be near me all the time, dating me after the relationship is established
   - touching me (i.e., holding hands, playing with my hair, small of my back)
   - being passionate for me. We will have a great sex life!
   - speaking often about how he feels about me to me and to others
   - speaking kindly to me. No passive-aggressive behavior.
   - being interested in all aspects of my life

- loving me for my innate goodness

3. Loves children—my own and his if he has any. He will show this by:

    - putting their needs above his own in a healthy way
    - playing with them, teaching them, reading to them
    - being patient most of the time
    - being openly affectionate

4. Has a great sense of humor. He will show this by:

    - making me laugh all the time, even when I am mad, and after making me laugh, he will pull me into his arms and onto his lap, whisper he loves me, and make me laugh all over again.

5. Is my partner. He will show this by:

    - In my business pushes me to do more, be my best. Encourages me.
    - Loves to do things with me because it is time with me, i.e., cooking, traveling, dancing, reading, watching thunderstorms, etc.
    - Can hold his own with my strong personality and is not easily intimidated by me.

After I finished writing my list, I realized that if this man were to exist (let's be honest, I didn't think it was possible), I did not feel I was currently the woman he would want. So, I wrote an accompanying letter to myself about the woman I wanted to become.

> Who I want to be for my future husband someday:
>
> I want to be a woman who sees and values her own worth. Is strong and fair. A hard worker. Has a strong testimony, honors her covenants, and has a personal relationship with her Savior. She is loving, kind, compassionate, and fulfills her church callings to the best of her ability. Faces things she is afraid of, with courage and faith that God can do anything. I will be a woman dedicated to maintaining my health to be a good example to my children, and to live a longer and happier life.

I will be financially independent and a wise steward of the money I am blessed with. I will be a woman who continues to work on developing her God-given talents.

I will be passionate, learn my future husband's love language, and speak it often, so he knows how much I love him.

I will be virtuous, saving myself for the bonds of matrimony. I will attend the temple frequently. Teach my children proactively and will love with my whole heart and soul.

After writing my letter to myself, I had a realization. The woman I described was pretty amazing. I did not feel like I was her yet, but I thought I could become her with the Lord's help. I realized that the woman I wanted to become was happy—and secure enough in herself to be happy being alone. Then, *if* someone did come into her life, he would be a bonus. But *if not*, she could be content and happy either way. This realization shifted my daily focus as I moved toward creating joy in my life. I began to strive to become a woman who was content and happy in her life just as it was, knowing with a clear surety that the Lord was at the helm.

Broken and Beautiful

"The Savior loves to restore what you cannot restore.
He loves to heal wounds; you cannot heal.
He loves to fix what has been irreparably broken." [12]

—Dale G. Renlund

The Japanese have a wonderful practice called kintsukuroi that imparts value to broken items. They repair these broken articles by gluing all the individual pieces back together and then filling in the cracks with gold or silver. Amazingly, the process makes the pieces even more beautiful for having been broken.

As I continued to focus on healing my heart, I could see the benefit of allowing myself the opportunity to mourn the loss of what had been so precious to me. I made no apologies for how I had felt. I did not wallow in self-pity, but I did acknowledge that I felt sorrow for which I had no solution. I asked the Lord, "Is there no balm in Gilead?"

Then I asked, "Is there nothing to heal the pain I feel?" As I asked these and many other questions, reassuring scriptures came as answers to my mind.

> And Jesus answering said unto them, They that are whole need, not a physician, but they that are sick.[13]

I did not feel whole. In my post-divorce moments, every part of me had felt broken, sick, and worthless.

> Have ye any that are sick among you? Bring them hither. Have ye any that are lame, or blind, or halt, or maimed, or leprous, or that are withered, or that are deaf, or that are afflicted in any manner? Bring them hither, and I will heal them, for I have compassion upon you; my bowels are filled with mercy.[14]

I had felt all that the Savior described. I wondered if the Lord would have compassion on my heart that had been maimed and torn apart. Would He recognize that I felt lame, stumbling along, only one half of what used to be a whole? Did He see my blindness to my faults? Did He understand that my self-worth had withered? Did the Savior know I felt deaf to anything that He had in store for the rest of my life? Would His bowels be filled with mercy toward me?

> And Jesus went about all the cities and villages, teaching in their synagogues, and preaching the gospel of the kingdom, and healing every sickness and every disease among the people.[15]

Did He *truly* understand how I felt and what I was experiencing? Would He heal this sickness in me?

> And he shall go forth, suffering pains and afflictions and temptations of every kind; and this that the word might be fulfilled which saith he will take upon him the pains and the sicknesses of his people. And he will take upon him death, that he may loose the bands of death which bind his people; and he will take upon him their infirmities, that his bowels may be filled with mercy, according to the flesh, that he may know according to the flesh how to succor his people according to their infirmities.[16]

The Son of Righteousness [shall] arise with healing in his wings.[17] The phrase "healing in his wings" caught hold in my mind. I envisioned the Lord carrying me in his arms, lifting, and healing my broken and sick heart. He became my "balm of Gilead." And with Him, I felt that I could do more than just survive my divorce; I could thrive! He, as the Master Healer, could heal my heart and bring me peace.

I pondered the scripture: "That their hearts might be comforted, being knit together in love, and unto all riches of the full assurance of understanding to the acknowledgment of the mystery of God, and of the Father, and of Christ."[18]

I realized that the phrase "having your hearts knit together" was more than just a nice idea or concept. When you live together, work together, have children together, and are sealed in the Lord's holy house, your hearts become intertwined—or knit—together.

Divorce meant having that knitting or intertwining ripped apart. When something is ripped apart in that way, it bleeds profusely. Only when I allowed the Savior into what was left of my poor, wounded heart did the Master Healer slowly knit my heart back together.

> And he commanded them that there should be no contention one with another, but that they should look forward with one eye, having one faith . . . having their hearts knit together in unity and in love one toward another.[19]

Even though I had felt shattered through my divorce, I grew to know that I could become whole once again through the Atonement of Jesus Christ. Becoming whole would happen as I knit my heart in unity with the Savior's. Then, that which was broken could be made whole and all the more beautiful for having once been broken. The Savior promised, "A new heart also will I give you, and a new spirit will I put within you: and I will take away the stony heart out of your flesh, and I will give you an heart of flesh."[20]

An understanding of how I could be healed helped me to accept and acknowledge the sorrow I had felt about the circumstances of my divorce. The analogy of receiving a new heart—one that was dedicated solely to the Lord—caught hold of my mind and took root in my soul. "And blessed are all the pure in heart, for they shall see God."[21]

As I grew in understanding, I continued to find peace. I learned that what my Savior desired from me—his daughter, Noelle—was real, heartfelt communication *every day*. Even in my moments of discouragement and anger at circumstances out of my control, He had always been there. Day after day, He heard my pleas. He always provided comfort, and while things rarely turned out the way I had hoped, I still came to know that the Lord was deeply aware of all my needs. As I put my faith in Him, I could trust that He would meet them. My sons and I were safely in His care.

"Put your trust in God and move forward with faith."[22]

—Gordon B. Hinckley

Lessons Learned: Chapter 2

1. Remember, you are still a family after a divorce. Families come in all types and sizes.
2. When you pray, expect the Lord to answer your prayers. Anticipate miracles. He desires to bless us in small and big ways in our lives.
3. The promises of our eternal covenants are ours to claim when we are obedient.
4. Falling out of love with a spouse takes time. Be as patient and compassionate with yourself as you would be with a stranger.
5. Medication can be used as a tool to continue making progress moving forward. (Consulting with a professional is vital.)
6. Be direct in asking for help from your ward family for the support you need.
7. Take a break before jumping back into the dating pool. Emotions take time to work through.
8. Grow comfortable being alone in your own company.
9. Have a clear picture of what you desire in a future spouse and what you desire in yourself Setting goals is helpful.
10. Talk to your Heavenly Father every day. Tell Him about the small worries of your heart; cry out to Him with all the extreme anger you are feeling—He wants it all. There is no such thing as something too big or small for our Father in Heaven.

"Be patient with yourself. Perfection comes not in this life, but in the next life. Don't demand things that are unreasonable, but demand of yourself, improvement. As you let the Lord help you through that, He will make the difference."[23]

—Russell M. Nelson

Chapter 3

Foundation in Christ

"If you have determined to live righteously, do not become discouraged. Life may seem difficult now but hold on tightly to the iron rod of truth. You are making better progress than you realize." [1]

—Richard G. Scott

Finding Direction and Purpose

Part of my ultimate healing meant I had to ask myself some hard questions and face some even harder truths about the hopes I'd had for myself. For good or ill, these hopes had shaped and determined a lot of my life choices. I recognized that I had held a very idealistic view of what I wanted my life to look like from the time I was young. The key to my plan of happiness was to marry a returned missionary (RM) and be sealed in the temple. I thought if I had those two things in place, everything else would come together, exactly as I imagined.

Life had instead thrown a few curveballs along my way to my "grand plan of happiness." I did manage to marry an RM in the temple but then struggled with the side effects of infertility and miscarriages for years. Eventually, I was able to give birth to three beautiful boys. Although the rigors of motherhood were more demanding than I had anticipated, and my ideal and reality had fewer crossovers than I would have liked, through it all, I had learned to accept the changes.

Now, as I arose out of survival mode and my grieving period over my divorce, I realized that I no longer knew what I wanted my life to look like. My "grand plan of happiness"' no longer existed. I had no clear idea of what my future would hold or what I wanted it to look like for the first time ever.

This awareness left me feeling like a reed in the wind that could be easily pushed in any direction. I did not have the same course and purpose anymore. I did have a testimony of the Savior and the healing power of the Atonement of Jesus Christ. Still, I realized that I had built my foundation on a false idea of happiness and a life that no longer existed if it had, in reality, existed at all.

This recognition left me feeling bereft. It occurred to me that I had become the proverbial foolish man somewhere along the path and built my house upon the sand. What I was feeling now was the ebbing of the tide, pulling me out with it.

> Therefore, whoso heareth these sayings of mine and doeth them, I will liken him unto a wise man, who built his house upon a rock—And the rain descended, and the floods came, and the winds blew, and beat upon that house; and it fell not, for it was founded upon a rock. And every one that heareth these sayings of mine and doeth them not shall be likened unto a foolish man, who built his house upon the sand—And the rain descended, and the floods came, and the winds blew, and beat upon that house, and it fell, and great was the fall of it.[2]

How could I have a testimony of Jesus Christ and His Atonement? How could I know that the Book of Mormon was true, translated by Joseph Smith, a prophet of God? How could I know and believe that we had a current living prophet today? How could I know all these irrefutable truths and more, yet still find myself on sand?

I did not have the answers, and my future was a blank page, a story yet to be written. I had to decide who the author ultimately would be. For years I had tried to write my own story, orchestrating every step, trying to keep myself and my family on the path to lead us home to our Heavenly Father. But where had all my efforts—all my striving, maneuvering, and employing—gotten me?

Did I have the home life I had envisioned? Had the relationship I'd had with my former husband been what I had desired? What about my children? Did they see a mother happy and fulfilled in her life? Was I making progress in who I desired to become, and, more important, who the Lord desired me to become?

The answer to most of these questions was "no." Many of my good-hearted efforts had unintentionally hurt some of the people I loved the most. *My* efforts had been in vain. I realized I had to find a new way of living, a new way of thinking, and doing things that meant it wasn't all about what *I* wanted, what *I* thought was best, especially if I desired a different outcome.

> And now . . . remember, remember that it is upon the rock of our Redeemer, who is Christ, the Son of God, that ye must build your

> foundation; that when the devil shall send forth his mighty winds, yea, his shafts in the whirlwind, yea, hen all his hail and his mighty storm shall beat upon you, it shall have no power over you to drag you down to the gulf of misery and endless wo, because of the rock upon which ye are built, which is a sure foundation, a foundation whereon if men build they cannot fall.[3]

Here was my answer. I needed to build a foundation centered in and on Christ.

Truthfully, if you had asked me before my divorce if I were living a life built on the foundation of Christ, I would have enthusiastically responded affirmatively. But through counseling and my twelve-step work, I realized that I had been relying on my merits alone. I was so busy *doing* that I had stopped *becoming.* I was like Martha.

> Now it came to pass, as they went, that he entered into a certain village: and a certain woman named Martha received him into her house. And she had a sister called Mary, which also sat at Jesus' feet, and heard his word. But Martha was cumbered about much serving, and came to him, and said, Lord, dost thou not care that my sister hath left me to serve alone? Bid her, therefore, that she help me. And Jesus answered and said unto her, Martha, Martha, thou art careful and troubled about many things: But one thing is needful: and Mary hath chosen that good part, which shall not be taken away from her.[4]

I, like Martha, had allowed the Lord to come into my home. I had even welcomed Him. But also, like Martha, I was running around needlessly "doing," in an effort to try draw closer to the Savior. I wanted Him to see how capable I was. What an excellent homemaker I was. What a good friend, wife, and mother. I wanted the Lord to see how good I was at serving others, obeying all the commandments, and managing my church callings. The list of all I was "doing right" went on and on.

I wanted the Savior to see that I was busy "doing" all He had asked of me.

But who was I *becoming* while I was busy doing?

I needed to become Mary. I *wanted* to become Mary: to sit at the Savior's feet and choose the "good part." I wanted to be more like the Lord, more like *my* Savior, Jesus Christ. I took to heart Elder Uchtdorf's counsel: "May I suggest you reduce the rush and take a little extra time to get to know yourself better. Walk in nature, watch a sunrise, enjoy God's creations, ponder the truths of the restored gospel, and find out what they mean personally. Learn to see yourself as Heavenly Father sees you-as His precious daughter or son with divine potential."[5]

As I pondered these truths, new understanding seemed to flood my mind. I stopped "doing" because I thought I was supposed to. I knelt and prayed, and had long conversations with God about my life and my family's future. I did not have any immediate or dramatic revelations over what was next for me. I felt a quiet peace as I slowly moved forward on the path I was on. I began to examine how my experiences made me feel, and I asked myself questions such as the following:

- Is this bringing me closer to my Savior?
- Can I feel the Spirit as I participate in this activity?
- What am I learning?
- How am I growing?

If I answered no to the first two questions, I cut that activity from my life. I became a ruthless editor of my own life. I did not apologize or try to explain my choices to others. I practiced kindly and firmly saying no to anything that did not help me draw closer to the Lord. I did not know what life had in store for me or who my Savior wanted me to become, but if something did not bring me closer to Him, then it was not worth my time.

Time had become my most precious commodity—time with my children, time on my knees, time in the scriptures, time in the temple—time *becoming* instead of just doing.

I asked God who I was and what He had in store for me. Then I began to listen, really listen, and what I heard astounded me. I started to record in my journal the answers I received to my prayers.

I wanted to remember them. I wanted to be able to reread them. Here is my journal entry describing one of the first answers to my prayers that I received at this time:

> *Noelle, thou art an elect daughter of our Heavenly Father. He is aware of the current burden you carry, the sorrow that fills your heart. He is pleased that you have come to Him in prayer and to seek His will for your future and the path forward for your children. Know that because of your obedience and faithfulness, everything that you have need of will be provided for you and your children. As you seek the Lord's will, His timing will be revealed to you, and you will know what is best for you and your children. When you are lonely, cry unto the Lord for comfort. He knows the ache of loneliness and can succor you in those moments you feel weak. When you are filled with sorrow, cry unto the Lord, and He will be quick to hear even the silent pleadings of your heart. Angels will attend and minister to you. You will be given strength beyond your own to do all that is required of you. This time of sorrow is not all that the Lord has in store for you. Soon your days will be filled with so much joy, it will be hard to comprehend. The Lord desires to give you all the blessings of your heart. You are a noble and righteous mother in Zion. You are leading your sons with love and teaching them essential gospel truths. You will be guided to know how to best help them in all they do. As you seek for understanding, the Lord will guide you in the ways you need to focus and concentrate your efforts.*

This answer to my heartfelt prayer was deeply personal to me and nothing short of miraculous. It resulted from a different way of praying, which led to a different kind of answer than I had ever received before. Now, when I would go to pray, I would kneel, speak my thoughts and feelings aloud, and pour out my heart to my Father in Heaven. Then, I would sit and listen, writing down the thoughts and impressions I received, having previously asked for guidance to remember the sacred words spoken to me.

Every time I knelt and prayed, the Spirit would testify of my worth as a woman and a mother. Days of doing this turned into months, and soon I filled an entire journal full of sacred answers to my prayers. As I look back now, I can see the fulfillment of

Elder Holland's promise: "God is eagerly waiting for the chance to answer your prayers and fulfill your dreams, just as He always has. But he can't if you don't pray, and he can't if you don't dream. In short, He can't if you don't believe."[6] Using this method to pray, I actively recognized the hand of the Lord in answering my prayers, as I exercised faith in Him and trusted in His plan for me.

Through the process I've described, I came to recognize that I had previously had a regular negative inner dialogue about who I was as a daughter of God. Now, as I prayed, I received powerful daily encouragement for the things I was doing right, and constant validation from the Spirit about myself as a woman and a mother.

I also received correction—but from such a kind, quiet voice, and with such love and concern, I felt encouraged and strengthened to move forward and do what I needed to do to make changes and repent. The quiet voice soon replaced the loud, demanding voice in my head, shouting that I was not doing enough or worthy. I began to feel more hope and peace in my life, more confidence in my day-to-day choices, and my ability to fulfill my children's needs.

I found that to receive these types of answers to my prayers, I needed to cultivate an environment where the Spirit was welcome. I purposefully began to examine everything I allowed into my thoughts and home. There was nothing left unchecked from music to movies and books to electronic media. I also became very intentional about whom I let into my home or who I spent time talking to on the phone or in person.

Sometimes I found it easy to make these adjustments. Music, for instance, was quickly managed. I chose music that was uplifting and made me want to sing aloud—songs that empowered me to shake off the dust of the past and move forward with purpose and direction. Books were also fairly effortless to alter. I avoided overly dramatized love stories or novels that had any vulgarity or graphic excerpts in them.

Movie choices required a more fine-tuning and thoughtful approach versus immediate changes. I had used movies and Netflix as an escape from reality when I did not need to work. My tendency to often seek escape was gently pointed out to me in response to my prayers. By numbing out and watching something, I did not have to experience some of the painful feelings that seemed to be constant companions for me in those days. As I grew and strived to be more like Mary (versus Martha), I felt my heart change, and I no longer had the desire to watch certain shows or spend as much time on streaming services.

I also began to listen to general conference talks each morning while getting ready for my day. The messages gave me something positive to focus my mind on and did not allow my thoughts to wander into territory over which I had no control—and believe me, that were a lot of territories! I tried to finish my days reading my scriptures and expressing gratitude in my nighttime prayers. I felt my faith in my Heavenly Father and His plan for my life, growing little by little.

Courage to Be Imperfect

"If I were Satan . . . I would keep women so distraught and distracted that they would never find calming strength and serenity . . . catching them in the crunch of trying to be superhuman instead of realistically striving to reach their individual purpose and unique God-given potential. We must have the courage to be imperfect."[7]

—Patricia Holland

My progress was painfully slow. Often, I impatiently thought my progress should look like a straight upward line ever drawing me closer to my Father in Heaven. The reality was that my line of progress was much more up and down, valleys and peaks, with a general direction of moving upward. Some days I did not feel like reading my scriptures or even getting on my knees to pray. There were days I was filled with fear for my future, and I ached for the physical touch and validation of my worth from a man, which ironically made me feel even more weak and worthless.

I was very honest about how I was feeling, especially in my counseling sessions. During "my mission," I told my counselor about one night where I had spent the better part of an evening on an online dating site. Driven out of my mind with so much loneliness, I began the process of filling out a profile, only to stop about halfway through. I realized it would not ease the pain I was feeling. Despite my half-hearted attempts to check out dating sites, I knew I did not honestly want to date anyone at this time. Somehow in those dark moments, I mustered the courage to stop, turn off my computer, and cry to the Lord instead.

Instances of intense loneliness became less frequent as time passed, and I began to create a new life full of positive things to occupy my days. Work became more fulfilling, and time with my children continued to be rewarding. I developed deeper relationships with friends, and I felt young again serving alongside the sister missionaries. Instead of a closed door, my life was starting to feel full of possibilities.

Service to others encouraged me to also take a mental break from focusing on my problems and concerns for a while. My acts of service were frequently small, such as making a treat for a friend or babysitting for a few hours. But in return, I felt an increased sense of gratitude for all the blessings I was receiving in my life daily. Helping others enabled me to break out of the cycle of self-defeat I had found myself in with the demise of my marriage. As my gratitude increased, I found contentment in Dieter F. Uchtdorf's instruction, "As we lose ourselves in the service of others, we discover our own lives and our own happiness."[8]

I also found that as I honestly addressed how I was feeling in my counseling sessions, whether good or bad, I was able to have more patience and compassion with myself by recognizing that for me, it was a journey. I was going to make mistakes and have setbacks, but I was also making progress. Becoming comfortable with being alone was not easy. It was an uphill climb, but step by step, I was becoming more confident, and I found myself more willing to embrace who I was becoming—through the Atonement of Jesus Christ.

As I continued my process of "becoming," I was sometimes torn between wanting to seek after the will and time line of my Heavenly Father, and wanting *my* way immediately. My prayers in those moments went something like this: "Heavenly Father, I don't want to pray today, I don't want to read my scriptures. I want to wallow about my circumstances, and I want my life to look different. Now! Please help me to instead seek after Thy will, to be patient, and to listen."

After reconciling with God, I would read my scriptures and pray, then listen for the words my Father in Heaven wanted me to hear. Never once in my prayers did I feel chastised for struggling and being honest about not wanting to do what I needed to do. Instead, I would feel an undeserved and incredible love and patience directed toward me as I plodded slowly along. Several times, as I read in the scriptures, I came across a reference that seemed to explain the phenomenon of unconditional love that I felt from my Savior.

> Therefore, is the anger of the Lord kindled against his people, and he hath stretched forth his hand against them and hath smitten them; and the hills did tremble, and their carcasses were torn in the midst of the streets. *For all this, his anger is not turned away, but his hand is stretched out still.*[9]

And again in 2 Nephi, the Savior states, "The Syrians before and the Philistines behind; and they shall devour Israel with open mouth. *For all this, his anger is not turned away, but his hand is stretched out still.*

"Manasseh, Ephraim; and Ephraim, Manasseh; they together shall be against Judah. *For all this, his anger is not turned away, but his hand is stretched out still.*"[10]

These scriptures quote Isaiah and can be interpreted in a variety of ways. However, as I read the phrase "his hand is stretched out still" and saw its repetitions, a meaning came into my mind. Even though these people had angered the Lord, He did not turn them away. His hand was reaching out to them, inviting them to come unto Him, to repent, to try again, to look forward to a new day. "His hand is outstretched still" became a promise to me. I was going to stumble and fall. I would make mistakes and need to repent, but the Lord is standing with his arms wide open to receive me the moment I turned toward Him. He is ever willing to forgive my human weaknesses. Through repentance, I could (and I can) have a fresh new start.

Temple Instruction

"As you draw nearer to the Lord, he will guide you to become the best version of yourself." [11]

—M. Russell Ballard

As my understanding of the Lord's unconditional love increased, I felt a greater pull to be in the temple. I began to attend with more frequency, even though attending the temple was not easy as a single mom working full-time. I made a goal to go two to three times a week. On days I went to the temple, I would get up at 4:30 a.m. to be able to attend a 5:30 a.m. session. The early session allowed me to get home just in time to wake my sons and help them get ready for school.

At first, I struggled to stay awake and alert in a session because I was so tired. My body would visibly relax the moment I sat down in the temple. Everything was quiet. No one was asking anything of me. No one was demanding my time or attention. I could set aside my worries and stresses for a brief moment and feel completely safe in a way that was unique to being in the Lord's holy house. The more I attended the temple, the more I craved the feeling of peace found only there. The sacrifice of sleep was worth the blessings I received in return.

As I watched and participated in each different temple session, I began to stay awake more easily, and I learned new things. The symbolism of the ceremonies, which previously had seemed awkward and foreign, became restful to my mind and spirit. For the first time, I was able to fully memorize all the aspects of the ordinances. I began to see the fruition of the promise from Elder Ballard, "The endowment is literally a gift of power . . . and our Father in Heaven is generous with His power."[12] Being able to mentally recite phrases from the ordinances and covenants gave me added strength and guidance throughout my day.

During the endowment sessions, I took great comfort in the men and women's separate seating placement. I recognized that we were individually responsible for our own covenants to the Lord. I was not dependent on a husband, nor was someone dependent on me as a wife. I began to think of the Lord as my partner in my life. As I turned to Him, He made up the difference where I fell short.

I was also blessed with increased strength and capability as I participated in the washing and anointing (initiatory) ordinances. I learned new ways I could counsel with the Lord and hearken to Him. I felt heard, uplifted, and validated as a woman and daughter.

Wendy Watson Nelson teaches, "When covenant women keep their covenants, they have greater access to the power of God. His power generates a decrease in stress, an increase in energy, more and clearer revelation for their lives, renewed focus, courage to make needed changes, an increase in patience, and more time for what matters."[13] This new awareness of strength and power as a woman and mother helped grow my self-confidence and trust in the Lord's promises. I knew that my family would be taken care of, and I did not have to know *how* that was going to happen. I could just trust that I was in my Heavenly Father's attentive care.

In the temple, my understanding grew of how Heavenly Father expects a man should treat a woman. I had greater clarity of men's and women's roles within the kingdom of God, and how we are individual but designed to work together as partners with God. I observed small acts of kindness and true love—sometimes through the instruction in a session, other times through my observations of couples as they interacted with one another. The love I saw was not storybook love but a love that exemplified charity—the pure love of Christ. I resolved that if I ever were to find love again, I would strive for what I saw exemplified in the temple.

Through pondering my covenants, I learned how to be a better friend, daughter, mother, and wife. And I practiced what I was learning in the current relationships I had in my life. Even though I was not now filling the role of a wife, I recognized that I could have done some things differently in my previous marriage. I sought to understand my part, accept responsibility, and learn different behavior patterns so I would not repeat the same mistakes. My greatest desire was to be a good example to my children and to teach them healthy behaviors.

Another outcome of my attending the temple was greater peace in dealing with my former spouse and any legal issues. Work problems and familial difficulties also seemed to melt away. I had more patience with my children, and I began to view my trials through a more eternal lens—when I regularly attended the temple.

Thomas S. Monson promises, "As we go to the holy house, as we remember the covenants we make therein, we will be able to bear every trial and overcome each temptation. The temple provides purpose for our lives. It brings peace to our souls-not the peace provided by men, but the peace promised by the Son of God when He said, 'Peace I leave with you, my peace I give unto you: not as the world giveth, give I unto you. Let not your heart be troubled, neither let it be afraid.'"[14]

Often I watched the women in my temple sessions and learned other interesting lessons. When endowment participants added their ceremonial robes onto their temple clothes, the women usually remained standing, waiting for all the sisters to get finished placing and tying their robes. This gentle act of waiting meant that not one sister was ever left standing alone. No one felt as though they were holding up everyone else in the session. The Spirit seemed to whisper to me in those moments that there was symbolism in what I saw with the example of these women. Just like them, I was never alone, and my "singleness" would not hold anyone else up. I could and would continue to progress as I kept *my* covenants and drew closer to my Savior.

As my understanding of the temple symbolism and compassion for others increased, I desired that everyone feel the joy and love that I felt. I wanted all to partake of the "fruit" and have the same experience that Lehi had:

> And as I partook of the fruit thereof it filled my soul with exceedingly great joy; wherefore, I began to be desirous that [all] should partake of it . . . ; for I knew that it was desirable above all other fruit . . . . I beckoned unto them; and . . . did say unto them with a loud voice that they should come unto me, and partake of the fruit, which was desirable above all other fruit.[15]

I began to ask what I could do to help others feel the love of the Savior while they were with or near me. I prayed to know how I could help them to taste the fruit of the Atonement of Jesus Christ. My heart was filled with the desire to be swallowed up in the love of the Savior. I wanted all who met me to feel the Savior's love for them, through their association with me. I prayed that He would consecrate my grief and pain and that He would turn my sorrow into something beautiful through the infinite power of the grace of Jesus Christ. More than anything, I hoped to become an instrument in the hands of the Lord.

"And they fasted much and prayed much that the Lord
would grant unto them a portion of his Spirit to go with them,
and abide with them, that they might be an instrument in the
hands of God . . . And the Lord said unto them also . . .
yet ye shall be patient in long-suffering and afflictions,
that ye may show forth good examples unto them in me,
and I will make an instrument of thee in my hands."[16]

Lessons Learned: Chapter 3

1. Build a foundation centered in and on Jesus Christ.
2. Work on who you are **becoming** versus a list of what you are **doing.**
3. Become a ruthless editor of your own life. Do not allow anything to take your time or effort if it does not bring you closer to your Father in Heaven.
4. Write down answers to your prayers. Create a sacred prayer journal.
5. Cultivate an uplifting environment in your use of music, books, media, etc.
6. Embrace your imperfections-this is how God strengthens us. Ether 12:27 tells us: "And if men will come unto me, I will show unto them their weakness, I give unto men weakness that they may be humble, and my grace is sufficient for all men that humble themselves before me; for if they humble themselves before me, and have faith in me, then will I make weak things become strong unto them."[17]
7. Serving others increases gratitude and provides a much-needed mental break from your own concerns.
8. We are given limitless chances. God continually extends the arm of mercy toward us, beckoning us to join Him.
9. Magnifying our covenants is a blessing to us and to others in endless ways.
10. Pray for your sorrow and grief to become consecrated for your good.

"The Final Judgment is not just an evaluation of the sum total of good and evil acts, what we have done. It is an acknowledgment of the final effect of our acts and thoughts—what we have become." [18]

—Dallin H. Oaks

Chapter 4
Healing and Forgiveness

"Greatness is best measured by how well an individual responds to the happenings in life that appear to be totally unfair, unreasonable, and undeserved." [1]

—Marvin J. Ashton

Ready to Receive

Despite feeling as though my heart was filled with the love of the Savior and desiring for others to experience the peace and joy I was feeling, I still had hard things to overcome and more lessons to learn, especially concerning forgiveness.

Right after my divorce was finalized, and shortly after we had moved into our rental home, I clearly remember a moment when I found myself standing in the middle of my closet. I stood with hands balled into fists, tears spilling down my face, as I tried to "will" myself to forgive my ex-husband. I was overwhelmed with feelings of grief. I felt deep sorrow over the loss of my marriage, my home, and my time with my children.

I pleaded with the Lord to help me forgive. I prayed, thinking forgiveness was the magic key to end all the heartache I was feeling. If I could just forgive him, I knew I would not hurt so much—I would be able to experience the peace I desired more fully in my life. Despite my pleadings, I could not forgive him that day.

I began talking with friends and family, asking them to reflect on times they had been faced with the difficulty of forgiving. What were their suggestions for me? Repeatedly, I heard that *time* was a huge part of the equation. I did not feel as though I had the luxury of time.

Even with all the growth I had experienced, I knew that I could not move forward toward a more productive life unless I could cross off "forgave him" on my mental checklist. I understood the principle of forgiveness on a logical level, but it was more of a theory than anything I was actively experiencing in my life.

Time went on. I continued to pray for the ability to forgive. I listened to talks on the subject, read my scriptures, fasted, and attended the temple. But real, heartfelt forgiveness continued to elude me. I had moments when I would feel my heart begin to soften, but no matter what I seemed to say or do, the feelings of goodwill would not stay with me for long.

I recognized the truth in Elder Hale's words: "In my life, I have learned that sometimes I do not receive an answer to a prayer because the Lord knows I am not ready. When He does answer, it is often here a little and there a little because that is all I can bear or all I am willing to do."[2]

Often during the occasions I prayed to be able to forgive, recollections of incidents that had wounded me caused me to feel justified in withholding my forgiveness. My inward reaction to my ex getting remarried was one of the episodes my mind replayed over and over again. In a previous chapter, I referenced a phone call during which he informed me that he would be remarrying, but I did not go into detail about what I was truly feeling. My private emotional reaction to his news was quite different from what I conveyed during that call.

The moment we hung up, tears welled up, and I softly whispered, "It isn't fair!" Once the words escaped my mouth, the rush of emotions fully hit, and I cried out in anguish, "It isn't fair! What he's asking isn't fair. I can't go a single day without breaking down in tears over the loss I feel, and he is getting *married*? How is that fair? How is this right? And now I have to write a letter to the bishop addressing his intention to remarry? Lord, how can you ask this of me?"

At that moment, I had felt utterly defeated. I knew I had followed promptings and listened to the whisperings of the still, small voice. I had a testimony of the miracles and tender mercies I had received due to my obedience. Still, despite all I had done to heal, I felt there was no relief from the constant emotional sorrow I was experiencing. My ex-husband's request for a sealing cancellation because he was remarrying such a short time after our divorce was especially painful.

I found myself falling into the easy trap of wanting to place the blame on someone else for the divorce—it was their choices, their actions, not mine. Counseling taught me that patterns of blame continue to promote a victim mentality. These thought patterns locked me into what felt like a mental prison, precluding me from true healing and forgiveness.

My heart softened a little listening to Elder Holland's advice: "Believe that people can change and improve. . . . If something is buried in the past, leave it buried. Don't keep going back with your little sand pail and beach shovel to dig it up, wave it around, and then throwing it at someone, saying, 'Hey, do you remember this?' Splat!

Well, guess what? That is probably going to result in some ugly morsel being dug out of your landfill with the reply, 'Yeah, I remember it. Do you remember this?' Splat! And soon enough everyone comes out of that exchange dirty and muddy and unhappy and hurt."[3]

As I struggled to get out of the metaphorical mud, I was temporarily attending my parents' ward. I asked to have my records moved permanently to that ward to enable me to hold a calling, but my request was denied. I was informed that if I wanted to hold a calling, I would need to attend church in the ward where I lived.

Going to church in my home ward meant I would have to attend church with my ex and his soon-to-be wife. The thought of attending church again with them was extremely hard for me to accept. I struggled with feeling resentment about the denial to move my records, on top of my general sadness and frustration. I added "denial" to my list of grievances, which justified my withholding forgiveness. To be frank, I felt that the Lord was asking too much of me. I had already given and sacrificed enough.

"Strong faith in the Savior is submissively accepting of His will and timing in our lives-even if the outcome is not what we hoped for or wanted."[4]

—David A. Bednar

Change of Heart

One day I heard a lesson in Sunday School that helped shift my perspective so that I was able to make substantial steps toward softening and changing my heart.

That day in class, we read in Doctrine and Covenants, and my heart was pricked as the verses were read aloud:

"Nevertheless, he has sinned; but verily I say unto you, I, the Lord, forgive sins unto those who confess their sins before me and ask forgiveness, who have not sinned unto death. . . .Wherefore, I say unto you, that ye ought to forgive one another; for he that forgiveth, not his brother his trespasses standeth condemned before the Lord; for there remaineth in him the greater sin."[5]

I understood the scripture, "I, the Lord, will forgive whom I will forgive, but of you, it is required to forgive all men."[6] But I felt deeply "sinned against." I fought the idea that the greater sin was in me for not forgiving. I questioned if my forgiveness meant that the person who had wronged me would not be held accountable for what they had done. Or would my forgiveness absolve them of their actions? From my point of view, my anger and lack of forgiveness felt justified.

I could not reconcile what I had read in the scriptures with how I personally felt. Then, the Sunday School teacher shared the story of Corrie Ten Boom, a Christian woman who had been imprisoned in a Nazi concentration camp with her sister Betsie. Their "crime" was hiding and protecting Jews. These are Corrie's words from her autobiography, *The Hiding Place.*

> When I was in the concentration camp, one of the most terrible things I had to go through was that they stripped us of all our clothes, and we had to stand [in front of the Germans]. The first time I had to do this, I said, "Betsie, I cannot do this!" And suddenly, it was as if I saw Jesus at the cross. And the Bible tells us they took His garments and He hanged there naked. And I knew He hanged there for me, for my sins! In my suffering, I understood a fraction of the suffering of Jesus Christ, and it made me so thankful that I could bear my suffering.[7]

At one of Corrie's many speaking engagements following the war, she shared another part of her story:

> It was some time [later] that I was in Berlin. There came a man to me and said, "Ah, Miss Ten Boom, I am glad to see you. Don't you know me?"
>
> Suddenly I saw that man. He was one of the most cruel overseers—guards—in the concentration camp. And that man said, "I am now Christian, I found the Lord Jesus. I read my Bible, and I know that there is forgiveness for all the sins of the whole world.

> Also, for my sins. I have received forgiveness for the cruelties I have done. . . . I have asked God's grace for an opportunity that I could ask one of my very victims' forgiveness. Fraulein Ten Boom—Will you forgive me?"
>
> I could not. I remembered the suffering of my dying sister through him. But when I saw that I could not forgive, I knew that I myself had no forgiveness! Do you know what Jesus said about that? "When you do not forgive those who have sinned against you, My Heavenly Father will not forgive you your sins."
>
> I knew. Oh, I am not ready for Jesus to come because I have no forgiveness for my sins. I was not able. I could not. I could only hate him.
>
> Then, I took one of these beautiful texts, one of those boundless resources, Romans 5:5: "The love of God is shed abroad into our hearts through the Holy Spirit who is given to us." I said, "Thank you, Jesus, that you have brought into my heart God's love through the Holy Spirit who was given to me. And thank you, Father, that your love is stronger than my hatred!"
>
> That same moment, I was free, and I could say, "Brother, give me your hand," and I shook hands with him. And it was as if I felt God's love stream through my arms! You've never touched the ocean of God's love as when you forgive your enemies! Can you forgive? No? I can't either. But He can!
>
> When He tells us to love our enemies, He gives, along with the command, the love itself.[8]

Silent tears ran down my face as I heard the words of a woman who had endured much worse than I ever had in my life. A seed of desire was planted in my heart not just to learn how the principle of forgiveness could work in my daily life, but to feel it in my heart. I quietly prayed to understand the doctrine on a heart level, not just intellectually, and for the first time, I began to earnestly *want* to forgive and not just because God required it.

After my request to move my records was denied, I considered not going back to church. However, after time spent attending my parents' ward and after learning from Corrie Ten Boom, I felt my reservoir of faith had begun to be refilled, and my heart softened. I knew I had enough strength to be able to attend church with my ex-husband and his fiancée.

I made the active choice to continue to attend church. Primarily, I wanted to be able to partake of the sacrament each week. I knew I desperately needed the power that comes from renewing my covenants weekly. And I needed a calling—a chance to serve the Lord. I was called as a teacher in the Relief Society. This calling was one of the tender mercies that made it easier to return to my ward. I felt the sisters valued my opinions and unique perspective. Serving as a teacher gave me a purpose and something to look forward to each week.

I reminded myself that my testimony was of the gospel of Jesus Christ, not of the people. I also recognized that despite their best intentions, members are fallible, and they make mistakes. We are all imperfect.

The choice to attend church with my ex and his soon-to-be wife was a unique decision on my part, but it was an important turning point for me. As I continued to work through feelings of forgiveness, it was important to me for my children to see that I knew the gospel of Jesus Christ is what enables us to do hard things. I wanted them to understand that ultimately if we follow the Savior, the rest does not really matter.

"Surely, each of us could cite an endless array of old scars and sorrows and painful memories that this very moment still corrodes the peace in someone's heart or family or neighborhood. Whether we have caused that pain or been the recipient of the pain, those wounds need to be healed so that life can be as rewarding as God intended it to be."[9]

—Jeffrey R. Holland

Real Desire

I continued to look for answers to rise above my struggles and feelings, and to move forward on a path of forgiveness. I slowly came to acknowledge that my frequent mental revisiting of frustrating historical episodes had stunted my ability to fully feel the healing effects of the Atonement of Christ and had delayed my personal progress.

Eventually, I came to believe Corrie Ten Boom's testimony that as we obey the command to forgive, the requisite love will follow. Forgiveness, I learned, is a process, not a one-time event. Developing a real desire to forgive was the first step in beginning that process. Neil T. Anderson further explains, "Don't wait until you feel like forgiving; you will never get there. Feelings take time to heal after the choice to forgive is made."[10]

My counselor helped me identify further steps I would need to take if I was going to change my mindset concerning my former spouse. Somewhere along the path, I had forgotten to think of him as a son of God. Instead, in my mind, he was a collection of all my injuries and sorrows.

Whether he intended to or not, his actions seemed to support my perception, which only reinforced my view of myself as a victim. The reality was that my perception of his actions could either be true or untrue. What he was choosing or not choosing to do in his life was not my business anymore. I was no longer responsible for any part of his eternal welfare. I was only responsible for *my* part, *my* thoughts, and *my* actions.

I began to pray daily to change the way I thought about my former spouse. When I thought of his words or deeds that seemed unkind, I would pray (aloud if I was alone), "God, please bless ___ with all the health, wealth, happiness, joy, and peace I desire for my own life."

In all honesty, the words initially tasted like ash in my mouth, as they certainly did not express how I felt. However, I knew from the personal revelation that this prayer was the place I needed to start. Having a routine prayer I could recite helped to retrain my mind not to dwell on endless mental loops of negative interactions with him. The prayer helped me break out of the frustrating, emotional cycle I had been circling.

As I worked to change my mindset, I took great comfort in Elder Holland's teachings on forgiveness: "He did not say, 'You are not allowed to feel true pain or real sorrow from the shattering experiences you have had at the hand of another.' Nor did He say, 'In order to forgive fully, you have to reenter a toxic relationship or return to an abusive, destructive circumstance.' But notwithstanding even the most terrible offenses that might come to us, we can rise above our pain only when we put our feet onto the path of true healing. That path is the forgiving one walked by Jesus of Nazareth, who calls out to each of us, 'Come, follow me.'"[11]

As I continued to pray to know what more I could do, the Lord answered that prayer through my bishop. At one of our appointments, he shared that he'd come from a divorced home. As a result, he had learned that parents speaking ill of a former spouse did not yield positive results with children. I had heard this advice before, but when it was coupled with stories from my bishop's own personal experiences, I resolved to never say anything about their dad that would cause pain for our children.

When my sons came to me with questions concerning the divorce, I answered with love and honesty. The kids' questions usually came in quiet evenings while I tucked them into bed. I would snuggle their little wiggly bodies and help them get comfortable. While stroking their sleepy faces, I would reassure them that even though Mommy and Daddy were not together anymore, they were deeply loved. They each were born out of love, and there would always be a part of me that loved their dad because he gave them to me. Then, I would whisper in their little ears that they were my greatest treasures.

Some of their questions during our evenings together reflected their concerns about a step-parent. I reassured my children that there was room in their hearts for *all* of us. Because of their ages, I likened their experience to a familiar story they loved, *How the Grinch Stole Christmas.* I emphasized a line toward the end that explained that the Grinch's heart expanded to make room for everyone. He did not have any "Who" he loved best; he loved them all. I taught my sons that their hearts could expand to make room for a step-mother. They did not need to decide who they loved best, just as Heavenly Father does not love any of His children best. He loves us all perfectly.

Sometimes I could not find the right words to answer all their questions. Other times there were issues best left unaddressed. At those times, I would tell them, "Your dad and I are still working that out." Usually, they would just file away my response and move on to the next item of most importance in their little lives. I knew they would have more questions at some point, but for now, these candid truths were enough for all our healing and growth.

As my children got older and their questions became more direct regarding the divorce, I encouraged them to simply look for the best in every situation. I frequently reminded them that they were my most favorite part of my marriage to their dad. I never wanted them to feel as though I regretted anything from that part of my life.

As I changed to this new way of thinking and speaking, I realized two important facts: First, truth is stronger than just a comforting phrase I might be tempted to tell my children. I struggled to admit those facts initially, but I was adamant that my sons know they were born out of love. They were not mistakes, nor was my marriage to their dad.

Second, children are designed to love both of their parents. Although I, on some level, had wanted my sons to choose me and my side over their dad's, I realized that I could not encourage my sons to make that choice. I knew that if I had done that, it would have been incredibly destructive for my children. God does not force us to choose or agree with His side or perspective. We are each given agency.

My realization of these facts affected how I spoke about my divorce with my children. As a result, we had more peace in our home, and I had a useful boundary for myself in how I chose to think of and speak about the father of my sons.

"We will receive the joy of forgiveness in our own lives when we are willing to extend that joy freely to others. Lip service is not enough. We need to purge our hearts and minds of feelings and thoughts of bitterness and let the light and the love of Christ enter in. As a result, the Spirit of the Lord will fill our souls with the joy accompanying divine peace of conscience." [12]

—Dieter F. Uchtdorf

Love of Christ

My progress toward understanding what forgiveness would look like in my life felt like a dance—two steps forward and one step back. Purging my heart and mind of bitter feelings to allow for the love of Christ to enter in (as Elder Uchtdorf counseled) became the next step I focused on.

I had to start by addressing some of the inherently difficult feelings that came as an aftermath of my divorce. These were the ugly, horrible thoughts and feelings I did not want to admit that I even felt, let alone ever state aloud. As I worked with my counselor, however, I learned that no matter how ugly and awful those thoughts were, they did not preclude my being loved by my Savior.

In contrast, I learned how Satan tries to turn good and genuine feelings into stumbling blocks. For example, I struggled with the natural feeling of loneliness after spending nearly two decades married. I wanted someone by my side with whom I could share my life. Companionship with a loving spouse is a good feeling.

Heavenly Father designed His children for marriage as husband and wife. Satan twisted my loneliness into a romanticized idea that I needed someone else to be "complete." In the moments when I was overcome with loneliness, I would pray aloud for help, openly admitting my weakness to the Lord and asking that He replace it with a love for others and a desire to serve.

By recognizing this weakness and depending on the Lord, Satan lost power to have any lasting effect on me in this area of my life. The feelings of loneliness did not go away completely for a long time. Still, by acknowledging how I was feeling about my loneliness, processing these feelings, and then asking for help, I could overcome it. I found that the principle of forgiveness worked in much the same way. I had to admit how I was really feeling toward a person or situation, ponder my feelings, and then plainly ask the Lord for help.

Again, there were moments when I did not want to pray or admit my feelings. Yet, as I strove to be authentic and admitted my reluctance as part of my prayer, line upon line, I built more spiritual muscle, and my heart continued to change. Kim B. Clark reassures us, "None of us are perfect. Sometimes we get stuck. We get distracted or discouraged. We stumble. But if we look to Jesus Christ. . . . He will lift us up . . . forgive us and heal our hearts."[13]

As one part of my heart started to change, I would have a new insight into a different area requiring more introspection. For example, I struggled with the idea that I no longer knew who I was spending the rest of my life with, let alone eternity. I felt angry at the outcome I was living but had not wanted. I developed feelings of bitterness and cynicism toward men and families in general. I felt as though I no longer had a place in a family-oriented religion, as I was not a part of a complete family anymore, at least not the one I had envisioned for myself.

When my sons and I had attended church in the beginning, I found myself looking around and feeling as though I was the only person experiencing any problems, especially as I saw other families sitting together, nicely dressed, with two parents and happy children all in a row. Everyone else appeared to have a perfect life. In comparison, I felt like a train wreck on display walking into sacrament meeting. Church was hard. Seeing happy families together was hard. Being alone was hard.

In my counselor's office, there hung an image of a hen gathering her baby chicks under her wings to protect and nurture them. I pondered that image week after week, and each time I felt the

Savior's love through His words: "O ye people . . . who are of the house of Israel, how oft have I gathered you as a hen gathereth her chickens under her wings, and have nourished you."[14]

I pictured the Savior gathering me into His arms, trusting that as I relied on Him, I would be given all that I needed. His words were like manna to my weary soul. The more I reached for Him in every thought, the more I began to graciously view those around me. My Savior's love filled my heart and changed my vision. I had new eyes to see those around me. I no longer saw "perfect" families. I saw individuals—men, women, children, teenagers, young and old—all needing the Savior, all striving to do and be their best.

My heart had begun to change, and I was filled with compassion toward all. I realized I was not the train wreck nor the victim I had believed myself to be. When I looked through the lens of my Savior's love, I saw a mom, a woman, a daughter of God trying to do her absolute best. I saw the truth in Elder Renlund's words: "The Church is like a big hospital, and we are all sick in our own way. . . .We must not only be tolerant while others work on their individual illnesses, we must also be kind, patient, supportive, and understanding as God encourages us to keep on trying. He expects us to also allow others the space to do the same at their own pace."[15]

So far, in my journey, I had learned that forgiveness is not merely something to cross off of a to-do list, nor is forgiving someone an act of absolving them of the hurt they have caused. Forgiveness is a process that refines us and creates a change of heart in us. It is letting go of grievances and old patterns of thought that are not beneficial. I likened my desire to forgive to a mustard seed of faith. If I could plant even the tiniest seed of desire to forgive, the seed would grow, and I could nourish it into something strong and beautiful.

About seven months after my divorce, I had a very sacred experience that taught me more about the principle of forgiveness. Late one Sunday night, I lay in bed, unable to sleep. My mind replayed unhappy scenes and words that had recently been exchanged between my former spouse and me. I had felt re-wounded after I had begun to heal. Discouraged, I prayed to be free of my distressing thoughts. After much difficulty, I fell lightly asleep, still praying for peace, but tossing and turning while I tried to reconcile my emotions. During this half-awake state, I saw in my mind's eye a dreamlike vision.

I was standing at the judgment bar of God. The Savior stood beside me and beckoned for me to watch. At that moment, I saw in front of me bits and pieces of my life go by. I recognized experiences from my past that had already occurred and then watched events unfold that I had yet to experience. I instinctively felt that, overall, my life had been very good, happy, and fulfilling. Then, another person was called, who now stood at the bar. No words were spoken, but I understood that they were there to be held accountable for the actions that had injured me. The Lord beckoned to me again, and I knew that justice would be served for all that I had suffered. However, the person at the bar seemed to be weighed down by the burden of guilt and seemed filled with sorrow, knowing that justice would be exacted. The Savior turned to me again, and I understood that I could choose to hold them accountable or to forgive them entirely. Once more, I reflected on my life. The scenes I had just experienced came into my mind again, and I could see that the Lord had not withheld a single blessing from me while on earth. My life had been rich and full, and I had even more to look forward to. My divorce was not the end for me. As I came to this understanding, my heart was filled with compassion toward the person at the bar, and I frankly forgave them every whit. I expressed to the Lord that I did not need any further compensation. The wonderful life that had been bestowed upon me more than made up for the sorrows I had experienced. My desire for justice left me. I felt free, light, and happy.

The scene closed from my mind. I awoke fully and fell from the side of my bed onto my knees. Tears came as I recalled the details of the dream. I prayed, asking that I might understand all that I had seen and experienced. My dream was an answer in response to my persistent prayers for the ability to forgive.

The intention of the dream was to give me hope. Through inspiration, I came to understand that while my desire to forgive was righteous, it would require more time. I needed to be patient and trust the Lord's timing. I felt reassurance and peace from the Spirit that I would be able to fully forgive *someday.*

My prayers were answered in a remarkable way! I understood that I would still need to work toward forgiving, but I would get there. That knowledge released the urgent need in me that I forgive immediately. It also helped me let go of the condemnation I felt toward myself for not being able to forgive promptly. From this experience, I learned to further trust my Father in Heaven. That trust moved me forward in my journey. I uttered another prayer of gratitude for my increased understanding.

"Be assured there is a safe harbor. You can find peace amid the storms that threaten you. Your Heavenly Father—who knows when even a sparrow falls—knows of your heartache and suffering. He loves you and wants what is best for you. Never doubt this." [16]

—Joseph B. Wirthlin

Lessons Learned: Chapter 4

1. Expect to receive answers to prayers only when you are ready.
2. Blame prevents healing and promotes a victim mentality.
3. With the commandment to forgive comes the *love* from our Father in Heaven to be able to do so.
4. People are not perfect. They make mistakes. Treat them with the same grace you desire for yourself.
5. Forgiveness is a process, not a one-time event.
6. You are responsible only for your thoughts and actions—no one else's.
7. Choose to not speak poorly of your former spouse to your children.
8. Don't ask your children openly or inadvertently to choose your side. If you need to pick a side, pick theirs.
9. Nothing you say or do will prevent you from the unconditional love of the Savior.
10. Forgiveness is a process of refinement. Trust the Lord in his timing.

"Somehow, forgiveness with love and tolerance accomplishes miracles that can happen in no other way."[17]

—Gordon B. Hinckley

Chapter 5

Forgiveness and Boundaries

"We do not know the hearts of those who offend us."[1]

—Henry B. Eyring

Healthy Boundaries with Family

My former spouse had a large family, and we used to meet together at least once a month to celebrate family birthdays, and spent all significant holidays together. Because most of the family all lived in the same area, grandparents and other family members often came to school activities, concerts, and sports events to show their support.

Before my divorce, as I tried to work through marital issues, I chose not to speak openly with my spouse's extended family surrounding our circumstances. I did this first out of loyalty to my husband but, more important, because at the time I was trying to leave a door open for reconciliation. The second reason was that on the one occasion I *did* try to have an honest conversation with my in-laws about some of the issues we were dealing with as a couple, the discussion was unproductive. Unfortunately, the conversation caused further hurt feelings on both sides.

As the relationship between my spouse and me deteriorated and divorce became imminent, I chose to continue to remain quiet about our personal circumstances with his extended family for my children's sake. Several family members cut ties with me entirely once the divorce was final. I felt as though I simply ceased to exist for them. I loved my spouse's extended family, and I genuinely grieved the loss of those relationships as well.

With help from my counselor, I realized that I had done my best under the circumstances. Instead, I turned my time and attention to learning all I could to encourage healing for myself and my children. I learned that healthy boundaries are an essential part of the process of forgiveness and healing.

I began to participate in an online group for divorced members of the Church. I found it helpful to see what other people had done in similar circumstances to mine. Online I found a wealth of knowledge available at my fingertips. Even more, I felt so much love and encouragement from the group members, a commonality I did not know had previously existed. Every type of example of relationships with extended family was available for me to learn from. I discovered that my situation was not unique. Here is a small representation of what was shared about in-laws. Out of respect to members, I have kept these comments anonymous.

- "My former in-laws don't talk to me or act like I exist. . . . It's hard."
- "I tried to let mine know that whatever happened between their son and me that my kids are still their grandchildren. . . . They do not call, or reach out to the kids. Unfortunately, they have exactly the relationship they have chosen to have with our children."
- "My former in-laws knew their son was not honoring his covenants and still chose to support his choices."
- "The last time I tried to talk to my former in-laws, my ex-mother-in-law swore at me."
- "I still talk to my ex-in-laws. They have said I will always be a part of the family. They see he is the one that made poor choices."
- "My ex-in-laws are non-confrontational. They just smile and pretend everything is always good."

While none of these examples are my story, I resonated with tenets of their experiences. I realized I could forgive former family members for choosing not to talk to me, and at the same time, I did not have to expect previous relationships to return to what they had once been.

I also learned that setting limits on these former relationships promoted healing for myself. "We cannot set limits on others . . . but what we *can* do is set limits on our own exposure to people who are behaving poorly; we can't change them or make them behave right. Our model is God...He does not really make [people] behave. God sets standards. He lets people be who they are and then separates himself from them when they misbehave. . . . Separating ourselves protects love because we are taking a stand against things that destroy love."[2]

As I focused on learning more about boundaries, I began to see examples in my scripture study that helped me better apply what I was learning in my daily life. The story of Korihor in the Book of Mormon became one of my favorite examples of setting active boundaries with Christ-like love.

Korihor was exceptionally good with words and had become convinced that the gospel of Jesus Christ was based only on the traditions of men. He taught in a way that was appealing and flattering to the people's vanity. Through persuasion, he convinced many people to abandon the truths of the gospel.

The scriptures tell us that he led away the hearts of many of the Nephite people. After having much success convincing the Nephite people of his views, he went into the land where Ammon was the high priest over an entire nation, which he had been instrumental in converting to the gospel of Jesus Christ.

When Korihor came into the land of the Ammonites to try to convince them that their beliefs were false, they responded more wisely than the Nephites had. They did not allow Korihor to preach in their cities (first healthy boundary).

They bound Korihor and took him before the high priest and chief judge. The people of Ammon did not try to punish Korihor themselves, but rather they followed the laws of the land (another healthy boundary). When Korihor was taken before the chief judge and high priest, they allowed him to defend himself.

Korihor used that time to convince the judges that there was no God and that the tenets they believed were false. He again used much flattery and eloquence, expounding all his beliefs, professing them to be irrefutable truths. After listening to Korihor, the high priest and chief judge had an interesting response.

> Now when the high priest and the chief judge saw the hardness of his heart, yea, when they saw that he [Korihor] would revile even against God, they would not make any reply to his words; but they caused that he should be bound; and they delivered him up into the hands of the officers, and sent him to the land of Zarahemla, that he might be brought before Alma and the chief judge who was governor over all the land.[3]

The fact that "they would not make any reply to his words" demonstrates another healthy boundary: they did not try to argue with Korihor. They rightfully determined that his heart was hardened to the truth. They followed the next level of their law and brought Korihor to the highest court in the land to be judged by a higher authority. The chief judge and high priest trusted that Korihor would be judged in a manner that was best for the people of Ammon and even for Korihor himself. (We will come back to Korihor's judgment again, so make a note of that last healthy boundary!)

In my life, I strove to model the same healthy boundaries I saw in the scriptures. I set my own limits and standards with former family members. I did not waste any mental or emotional energy trying to rekindle relationships or to convince others of my side of the story. By setting these limits, I experienced much more peace in my life. Occasionally, I would run into past family members who were not speaking to me or hear a story told from their limited perspective of events. However, when I would experience these negative encounters or remember past ones, I would mentally pray, "Heavenly Father, help me to let go of my resentments. Help me feel the love that You have for each of them as your child. Please bless them with the health, prosperity, and happiness I desire for my own life."

In this way, I trained my mind and thoughts to focus on positive feelings instead of discouraging ones. Training my mind took time, and sometimes I needed a good cry before I could pray for my former extended family. However, I found so much more peace praying for them instead of dwelling on my grievances.

Divorce affects every extended family differently. It is natural to want to strive for the ideal, where all the parties are mutually respectful and kind to one another. But it's important to acknowledge that when you do *not* have the ideal relationship with former family members, you can still feel Christ-like love for those individuals and have healthy boundaries that promote healing for both parties. Larry J. Echo Hawk lovingly enjoins, "Brothers and sisters, are there people in our lives who have hurt us? Do we harbor what seem like fully justified feelings of resentment and anger? Are we letting pride keep us from forgiving and letting go? I invite all of us to forgive completely and let healing occur from within. And even if forgiveness doesn't come today, know that as we desire and work for it, it will come."[4]

In addition to setting appropriate boundaries for myself with former family members, I have chosen to be solely responsible for building and promoting my children's relationship with my own family. I have also encouraged the building and promoting relationships with my former in-laws and extended family to be my ex-spouse's responsibility.

We then are each responsible for the relationships within our own families. Also, out of respect for those relationships, I do not speak ill of my former extended family to my children. This guideline continues to facilitate healthy boundaries and promotes peace in our home.

"Choose to focus on things that fill your soul with hope."[5]

—Dieter F. Uchtdorf

Healthy Boundaries with Friends

Communications with former in-laws weren't the only interactions I had to learn to carefully navigate after my divorce. Circles of acquaintances and overlapping friends presented an especial challenge.

One day I ran into a friend in a local store parking lot. I had not seen her in almost a year. She casually asked how I was doing. Feeling emotionally raw that day and caught unprepared by her innocent questions, I did not know how to immediately respond. I ended up blurting out too many personal details about what was happening with the divorce and my kids. As I spoke, I could feel myself cringing inside and simultaneously wanting to slap a hand over my mouth to stop myself from saying anything more.

My friend was surprised at the news and (I am sure) at the volley of information I had just shared. I felt embarrassed by my lapse of judgment in the moment. My behavior revealed a need to learn how to handle unexpected questions and situations with more grace and dignity.

I repented of my words in that encounter and prayed for help to have a more Christ-like response in the future when others asked about my family. In counseling, I sought and learned some practical tips on simple yet truthful lines of dialogue to practice.

I learned that directness was the best approach when I was asked about my family. If someone was unaware of our divorce and asked about my husband, I responded that he and I were no longer married. Usually, the person would respond with apologies.

Sometimes they asked what had happened. My standard reply was that we were keeping the details to ourselves for the sake of our kids. Then I generally changed the subject to something more neutral such as activities in which my children and I were lately involved.

On the rare occasion that someone persisted in asking more questions, I would reply, "I am just taking it one day at a time and spending a lot of time on my knees." This response also worked well for the people who knew the circumstances of my divorce and asked with sympathy about how I was doing.

During each interaction, I tried to emphasize the hopeful versus the hurtful in my life. These types of replies were usually enough that people did not ask any more prying questions. I felt liberated when I did not have to pretend I was fine when I was not—emphasizing the hopeful also generally deterred some people from asking questions merely for the sake of gossip. I learned that I did not owe anyone an explanation.

I found that an important skill lay in recognizing the difference between healthy venting and emotional dumping. I often felt overwhelmed and needed to talk to someone about all that I was experiencing. I processed many feelings by talking about them aloud (sometimes to myself). But, I was blessed during this time with several good friends who were put in my life at exactly the right moment to help by being good listeners.

These women lived out of my immediate ward and neighborhood and therefore were unencumbered with intimate knowledge of the people, places, or things I referenced. As a result, they also were less emotionally invested in those details. They allowed me to call at any time, day or night, and always provided a shoulder to cry on.

Healthy venting to these strong women put me in a position to receive their constructive feedback and take positive actions. My friends encouraged me to look toward my future fearlessly and, when I was feeling my very worst, put on a great red lipstick, my best heels, and hold my head high regardless of what anyone else thought about me. Even though these suggestions may seem small, they helped me continue to move forward with confidence during trying times.

Another benefit of having an outlet in these friends was that they acted as a metaphorical pressure valve. I could vent my feelings to them and thereby avoid repeating the embarrassing situation when I revealed far too many personal details.

The people who needed to know the details of my life already did. These friends also made it easier to filter what I posted online and even what I conveyed in my private communications concerning my divorce. I realized I did not owe anyone any further explanation for my choices. I knew the Lord was pleased with my efforts, and, at the end of the day, His opinion was the only one that mattered.

Forgiving Myself

"Sometimes, of all the people in the world, the hardest to forgive—as well as perhaps the one who is most in need of our forgiveness—is the person looking back at us in the mirror."[6]

—Dieter F. Uchtdorf

The idea of forgiving myself caused a jumbled-up tangle of emotions. There were many aspects to all those emotions, and I worked with trusted professionals and others who knew and loved me to help unsnarl what I needed to forgive. Here are just a few examples:

- I needed to forgive younger Noelle for not knowing better.
- I needed to forgive myself for not having had better boundaries.
- I needed to forgive myself for not having trusted the Lord.
- I needed to forgive myself for wanting things my way.
- I needed to forgive myself for allowing others' opinions to determine my sense of my worth.

If I dissected every aspect of these issues, the discussion would fill an entire book by itself! I will touch on a few of my own realizations and how they related to my journey of healing and forgiveness.

Younger Noelle was the version of me who wanted the ideal in every facet of her life: the perfect marriage, complete with date nights every week. All of my children happy and valiant in the gospel. I would have a beautiful home, stability with work, and so on. I came to recognize that my ideals were not necessarily bad, and some of them were even still valid.

However, my narrow definition of what they should look like had limited my ability to grow into the woman the Lord desired me to become and slowed my progress. Most of the ideals I had were based on what was generally accepted within the culture of the Church or, to borrow a phrase from the scriptures, "the traditions of my fathers" (Galatians 1:15). Part of forgiving myself included embracing the fact that Heavenly Father's plan for me looked different from the one in my head, and acknowledging that His plan really was the perfect plan for me.

I recognized that I had done the best I knew at the time. When I learned better through experience, counseling, and twelve-step work, I earnestly tried to do better. In this way, I grew line upon line, discovering what God had in store for me. As my understanding increased, I came to have a testimony that His plan was so much better than any "ideal" I could ever create. I also discovered the immense freedom that came when I stopped trying to micromanage every aspect of my life and simply allowed the hand of the Lord to be revealed. This shift in thinking dovetailed with the promises found in the scriptures that are offered to those who strive to be covenant-keepers.

> And never could be a people more blessed than were they, and more prospered by the hand of the Lord. And they were in a land that was choice above all lands, for the Lord had spoken it.[7]

> Nevertheless . . . being strengthened by the hand of the Lord, having prayed mightily to him that he would deliver them out of the hands of their enemies; therefore the Lord did hear their cries, and did strengthen them.[8]

Frequently the scriptures refer to the Lord's lifting and sustaining hand in blessing His covenant people. These people were not perfect, but they were doing their best. As a result, they readily recognized the hand of the Lord in their lives, even when waiting for the Lord to "deliver them out of the hands of their enemies" (Isaiah 28:12).

This constant awareness of the Savior's promises to His people is a sharp contrast to the adversary's deceitful promises. The end of Korihor's story is a perfect example of Satan abandoning those he has led away from the safety of the gospel. (I told you we would come back to Korihor!)

> And Korihor did go about from house to house, begging food for his support. And it came to pass that as he went forth . . . among a people who had separated themselves from the Nephites. . . . Behold, he was run upon and trodden down, even until he was dead. . . . Thus we see that the devil will not support his children at the last day, but doth speedily drag them down to hell.[9]

Over and over, the scriptures testify that God keeps His promises. That does not mean life will not be difficult, but it does mean that He will not forsake us. He will deliver us in His perfect timing. There are no such promises from Satan. Ezra Taft Benson gently reminds us:

> God is mindful of you. He has given you commandments to guide you, to discipline you. He has also given you your agency—freedom of choice—to see if you will do all things whatsoever He shall command. Satan is also mindful of you. He is committed to your destruction. He does not discipline you with commandments but offers instead freedom to "do your own thing," the freedom to rebel against the counsel and commandments of God.[10]

Through counseling, I had learned to set better boundaries with others, including my former spouse's extended family and friends and acquaintances. But I also realized that I needed to learn and practice living with better boundaries in my personal life.

When it came to practicing forgiveness, I kept hearing trite advice such as "forgive and forget" or "turn the other cheek." I was also reminded of the Savior's admonition to forgive "until seventy times seven."[11] The command to forgive "seventy times seven" is often explained as symbolic, not literal, as the numeral seven is a religious representation of perfection. However, if that understanding is applied to the above scripture, it suddenly reads, "Thou shalt forgive him perfectly."

I found these expressions and admonitions demoralizing and often difficult to apply to others, especially while striving to maintain my own personal healthy boundaries. They were particularly confusing during my attempts to rebuild feelings of self-worth. I mentally berated myself for not being able to "turn the other cheek" or "forgive and forget perfectly" the issues concerning my divorce.

For example, I wondered, what do you say to a woman who has experienced any type of abuse: financial, physical, sexual, mental, or emotional? How is she be expected to "forgive and forget"? How does she establish healthy boundaries while "turning the other cheek"? How is she expected to be able to forgive others "perfectly"? These expressions became figurative stumbling blocks to my progress.

Not having these answers led me to start asking some hard questions on a doctrinal level to understand what my Father in Heaven was really requiring concerning forgiveness. I found Doctrine and Covenants Section 98:39–48 to be instructive:

> And again, verily I say unto you, if after thine enemy has come upon thee the first time, he repent and come unto thee praying thy forgiveness, thou shalt forgive him, and shalt hold it no more as a testimony against thine enemy—
>
> And so on unto the second and third time; and as oft as thine enemy repenteth of the trespass wherewith he has trespassed against thee, thou shalt forgive him, until seventy times seven.
>
> And if he trespass against thee and repent not the first time, nevertheless thou shalt forgive him.
>
> And if he trespass against thee the second time, and repent not, nevertheless thou shalt forgive him.
>
> And if he trespass against thee the third time, and repent not, thou shalt also forgive him.
>
> But if he trespass against thee the fourth time thou shalt not forgive him, but shalt bring these testimonies before the Lord, and they shall not be blotted out until he repent and reward thee four-fold in all things wherewith he has trespassed against thee.
>
> And if he do this, thou shalt forgive him with all thine heart; and if he do not this, I, the Lord, will avenge thee of thine enemy an hundred-fold;
>
> And upon his children, and upon his children's children of all them that hate me, unto the third and fourth generation.
>
> But if the children shall repent, or the children's children, and turn to the Lord their God, with all their hearts and with all their might, mind, and strength, and restore four-fold for all their trespasses wherewith they have trespassed, or wherewith their fathers have trespassed, or their fathers' fathers, then thine indignation shall be turned away;
>
> And vengeance shall no more come upon them, saith the Lord thy God, and their trespasses shall never be brought any more as a testimony before the Lord against them. Amen.[12]

I pondered these scriptures for a few weeks to really comprehend what the Lord was saying. Finally, I got it! I cannot express the relief and the peace that came into my heart when I began to understand. In verses 39–43, we are given the commandment to forgive even when someone else has not repented. Then, in verse 44, we learn that if these wrongs continue to be committed against us, we have the right to petition the Lord by bringing our testimonies to Him. ("But if he trespass against thee the fourth time, thou shalt not forgive him, but shalt bring these testimonies before the Lord.")

At this point, the Lord explains that the sins committed against us "shall not be blotted out." Or, in other words, the Lord punishes unrepentant repeat-offenders. Understanding this doctrine is so important, especially for someone who has, for example, endured repeated abuse of any kind.

We are not required to forgive over and over simply and blindly, but we are to bring all our sorrows and grievances to the Lord. He will remember our suffering and forgive that person only when they repent. We are also promised we will be rewarded more than what was done to us "four-fold wherewith in all things he has trespassed against thee."

The scriptures do not state how we will be rewarded, but we know with surety that God keeps His promises: "I, the Lord, am bound when ye do what I say; but when ye do not what I say, ye have no promise."[13] When we are doing our best to keep our covenants, the Lord is determined to hear our cries, the petitions of our heart, and to ensure that we are rewarded for what we have endured. But that is not all! "And if he do not this [repent] I, the Lord, will avenge thee of thine enemy an hundred-fold."

This scripture clearly states that the Lord Himself will avenge us. He will make sure there is justice for the wrongs that have been done against us. We worship a God who keeps all His promises. I cannot comprehend with my mortal mind what being avenged "an hundred-fold" would look like, but I have confidence in the Lord's promises.

Many of my unhealthy boundaries were tied up in seeking equality or fairness to find justice for what I had experienced throughout my life. This scripture block helped me understand that I could leave all my worries to the Lord. *God was on the job.* I did not need to fight a battle for compensation any longer. I could trust Heavenly Father's authority and righteous judgment, just as the chief judge and high priest trusted that Korihor's fate would be fair according to his deeds. (So many great lessons about healthy boundaries!)

The remaining verses in Doctrine and Covenants 98 continue to describe that the Lord's vengeance will be passed through generation upon generation unless they all turn to the Lord, repent, and make reparations for what was done. I love that the end result of His vengeance is mercy.

The Lord makes a provision for those who are willing to repent and turn to Him. If I am the one who has caused harm, even unknowingly, that same gift of mercy can also be mine, through repentance. Isn't that a beautiful gift? Elder Uchtdorf reassures us, "The merciful will obtain mercy."[14]

The other commonly heard phrase that produced a lot of misunderstanding and guilt for me was, "Forgive and forget." This motto is not actually found in the Bible but has made its way into our cultural lexicon and is often reported to have come from scripture. In actuality, it is found in Shakespeare's play *King Lear*, as the title character tosses out, "Pray you now, forget and forgive!"[15]

While Shakespeare has much of value to say, I trust the Lord's words most: "Behold, he who has repented of his sins, the same is forgiven, and I, the Lord, remember them no more."[16]

This scripture clearly states that it is *the Lord* who will remember our sins "no more." Furthermore, the Lord's remembrance of sins committed is dependent on the condition that the person has sincerely repented. We have been commanded to forgive everyone, but the Lord expects us to also use good judgment in how we choose to remember.

Remembering enables us to respect and protect healthy boundaries. We don't need to remember to re-wound or "throw mud," as Jeffrey R. Holland stated. However, we do need to judge righteously to maintain healthy boundaries. Thankfully, the outcome of the final judgment is not ours to make. Only the Lord can look upon the heart of someone and know if it is penitent.

Dallin H. Oaks clarified this principle when he taught, "I have been puzzled that some scriptures command us not to judge and others instruct us that we should judge and even tell us how to do it." He suggests that there is no contradiction between these scriptures if we (1) "understand that there are two kinds of judging: final judgments, which we are forbidden to make, and (2) intermediate judgments, which we are directed to make, but upon righteous principles."

Elder Oaks finishes with the helpful thought:

> This life is not the time for final judgments; those are reserved for the next. Additionally, we will not be in the position of making those final judgments; they are reserved for the Lord. Instructively, Jesus Christ Himself withheld such final judgments from many whom He could have condemned, such as Pontius Pilate, Herod, the woman at the well, the woman taken in adultery, and even Judas Iscariot.[17]

A close friend of mine demonstrated an example of protecting and respecting boundaries while exercising righteous judgment prior to her own divorce. Her husband had had an affair with another woman for an extended period of time. When they were trying to work through this and other marital issues, she realized that she could eventually forgive him for not honoring and keeping his covenants, but it was equally important that she not forget his prior behavior as a healthy personal boundary.

I think when discussing forgiveness and healthy boundaries, it is important to also remember Elder Holland's counsel: "To forgive does not mean we must re-enter a toxic relationship. That is not what our Father in Heaven desires of us." It is important to acknowledge that you can forgive someone and still remember their actions as a future safeguard to keep yourself from falling back into unhealthy patterns of behavior.

Tyler G. Griffin encourages us to remain focused on our Savior while making these "intermediate judgments." He states:

> Our own sins and lack of perfect understanding disqualify us from being able to pass final judgments on anyone, including ourselves. We must, however, make constant intermediate judgments. We are to righteously judge actions, not condemn people. When those judgments are based on principles of righteousness, our focus will more fully turn to the Lord Jesus Christ. We will increasingly rely on His perfect judgment, mercy, and grace rather than on mortal accomplishments or imperfections as a basis for judging God, ourselves, and those around us.[18]

Moroni, in the Book of Mormon, gives us an excellent guideline for practicing righteous judgment of others and for ourselves: "Wherefore, I show unto you the way to judge; for everything which inviteth to do good, and to persuade to believe in Christ, is sent forth by the power and gift of Christ; wherefore ye may know with a perfect knowledge it is of God."[19] Once I finally understood the small differences between what is culturally accepted and what is doctrinally correct, I made substantial progress forgiving myself and understanding the importance of having and maintaining strong boundaries.

In my journey toward forgiveness, I developed a strong testimony that we must have a change of heart and *want* to forgive. We cannot view forgiveness as something to cross off of a checklist. I also learned that boundaries are essential for healing and to allow God to hear my cries for justice and to fight my battles. I needed to trust that He will take care of it all!

I learned that there is a strength that comes from being alone, sitting with grief, and allowing myself time to heal and to forgive. I learned that trusting our loving Father in Heaven will make all things turn for our good, even the ugly bits that are uncomfortable and hard to face. All of it can work together for our good.

I wish I could say that my path toward forgiving others was smooth and that because of the amazing spiritual experiences I had been blessed with, forgiveness was all done and completed. But the reality is that my journey toward forgiveness is ongoing and has been a messy, uphill climb most of the time. I have learned that forgiveness takes time; it is a process—not a finish line.

The adversary understands that there is joy and peace to be found in forgiveness as we partake of the cleansing and healing power of the Atonement of Jesus Christ. Therefore, he will do anything to make our path more difficult. As covenant-keepers, we can feel for others a portion of the love our Savior feels for them. This love is what enables us to desire to forgive. It is a portion of the Savior's grace. Forgiveness, then, is not the ending of our story—it is only the beginning.

"Lay your burden at the Savior's feet; let go of judgment. Allow Christ's Atonement to change and heal your heart. Love one another. Forgive one another."[20]

—Dieter F. Uchtdorf

Lessons Learned: Chapter 5

1. Healthy boundaries are an integral part of the process of forgiveness and healing.
2. Do not chase after people or waste time trying to explain your circumstances to those committed to misunderstanding you. Everyone is on their own journey.
3. Choose not to speak ill of former extended family members, no matter their actions. When you do not have the ideal relationship, you can still feel Christ-like love for those individuals and have healthy boundaries that promote healing for both parties.
4. When someone asks why you got divorced, give yourself permission to say less.
5. Take things one day at a time. When you know better, do better. Emphasize the helpful versus the hurtful that is happening in your life.
6. Learn the difference between healthy venting and emotional dumping. Healthy venting serves a purpose and promotes positive actions.
7. Forgiving *yourself* is a process that takes time. Be patient and kind to yourself.
8. Heavenly Father's plan is better than any other plan. Trust that he can take the messy parts and turn them for *your* good.
9. You can forgive someone and still remember their actions as a future safeguard to keep yourself from falling back into unhealthy patterns of behavior.
10. Blessings follow obedience. The timing may be different from what we expect or even want, but the Lord *always* fulfills His promises.

"The Lord's delays often seem long, some last a lifetime. But they are always calculated to bless . . . Although His time is not always our time, we can be sure that the Lord keeps His promises."[21]

—Henry B. Eyring

Chapter 6

Steadfast and Immovable

"How do you remain 'steadfast and immovable' during the trial of faith? You immerse yourself in the very things that helped build your core of faith: you exercise faith in Christ, you pray, you ponder the scriptures, you repent, you keep the commandments, you serve others. . . . With faith come trials of faith, bringing increased faith."[1]

—Neil L. Andersen

Be Ye Not Deceived

While I was making significant steps forward in my healing journey, I was still trying to determine what some of my future plans would look like. It had now been a year since my divorce, and I considered joining the dating scene. My indecision about my desires for the future created a lull in my progress. So, Satan, the author of confusion, stepped in and used my divorce to sow seeds of doubt and discouragement in my mind.

I found myself questioning my idea of what it really meant to be a covenant-keeping woman. I originally envisioned this woman as someone who has been married in the temple, attended church weekly, fulfilled her callings, served regularly, went to the temple at least monthly, nurtured her family, read her scriptures, prayed daily, and more.

However, if a covenant-keeping woman is defined solely by these criteria, particularly when eternal marriage is part of the list, what did that mean for me as a divorced mother? Or, for that matter, what did it mean for anyone who finds themselves with a broken eternal marriage?

I began to doubt that I was living the gospel "right." I tried to combat the negative voices and thoughts by continuing with the typical Sunday School answers. I pictured my path forward in the Church as straight and narrow with my covenants placed like rungs on a metaphorical ladder, allowing me to ascend upward.

I knew the desire of my heart was to be a covenant-keeping woman, but I no longer fit the ideal of that woman in my own head. I began to think that because of my divorce, I was now stuck on a rung, unable to climb further until I was once again married in the temple. (What if that never happened again in this life?) And even worse, I wondered, did my divorce now mean that I was suddenly demoted down a rung?

Satan began to whisper: "Eternal marriage does not exist for you. You already failed at it. Look around. Everyone else is getting it right and sees that you are doing it wrong. Your ex-husband is happier without you. You are alone, and no one wants to be with you." Each time I slipped through my own expectations or by forgetting to read my scriptures or not praying morning and night, I felt I was falling short. Satan was right there, whispering, "This is too hard. No one else seems to be struggling like you are." I began to feel discouraged at my lack of progress and struggled to find happiness as I futilely strived to climb the mental "rungs of the gospel ladder."

Elder Peter M. Johnson taught, "The adversary . . . is aware of who you are. He knows of your divine heritage and seeks to limit your earthly and heavenly potential by using the three Ds: deception, distraction, [and] discouragement."[2]

The falsehoods of Satan continued with questions that had no easy answers: "What kind of loving God has you struggle so much to get closer to Him? This should be easier. Maybe there is an easier way. Look at what other people are doing. How are they living their lives? They look happy. You are not happy. This church doesn't make you happy. Doesn't God want you to be happy? A loving God would want you to be happy. You should do what makes you happy."

I felt overwhelmed with discouragement, even in the midst of doing all the "right things." I desired to remain close to my Father in Heaven, to become all He saw for me, but I was beginning to feel continued progress was impossible. In my downheartedness, I became more susceptible to the enticing's of the adversary.

With patient planning and cunning, Satan carefully directed my thoughts onto a subtly different path. His deceptions happened so slowly and incrementally that I could not discern the truth from the lies. Then, at the perfect moment, Satan presented me with everything I thought I ever wanted. "And he leadeth them by the neck with a flaxen cord, until he bindeth them with his strong cords forever."[3]

The first flaxen cord of the adversary that twined round my heart began with a good friendship that soon developed into feelings of genuine mutual admiration. I cared deeply for this person, though our values were not the same. While we were not formally dating, I could not seem to stop investing emotionally in the relationship. I had even begun to make little concessions here and there and was rapidly losing ground in standing firm in my convictions. I logically understood the friendship was not the best thing for me and prayed for strength to walk away. I knew deep down I could not have the future I desired with him.

After months of struggling, a simple phone call helped me make a final decision about the path I really wanted to be on. I had bought into the lie that if I chose not to make any decision one way or the other, I was still in safe territory. During this particular call, this friend finally confessed the depth of his feelings, even going so far as to profess his love for me. He asked me to meet him at a hotel for the weekend. He reasoned that if we both loved each other, what was the harm in showing it? We were both consenting adults. We could enjoy sex with no strings attached.

I paused to absorb what had been offered. On the one hand, my heart was thrilled that this person (for whom I had been secretly pining) confessed that he loved me. And I had felt the ache of loneliness daily. The desire to say yes was overwhelming because I desperately wanted to feel loved and desired by someone. This friend was smart. He was funny. He had given me great advice on more than one occasion. He had been there for me through some really difficult times.

A quote from *Jane Eyre*, one of my favorite books, came into my mind as I wrestled with the decision before me:

> I will keep the law given by God; sanctioned by man. I will hold to the principles by me when I was sane, and not mad—as I am now. Laws and principles are not for times when there is no temptation: they are for such moments as this, when body and soul rise in mutiny against their rigour; stringent are they; inviolate they shall be. If at my individual convenience I might break them, what would be their worth?[4]

His offer of love seemed to promise everything I had ever wanted, and I very nearly said yes.

I recognized that at that moment that like Jane Eyre, I was not "sane." I was overcome in my mind with the desires of my heart. I felt the mutiny of body fighting with soul for dominance, and I silently prayed for strength. As I stood in the middle of my bedroom, I received a power that was not my own. Wendy Watson Nelson explains, "[When we] let our covenants influence our thoughts and words and actions, we are inseparably connected to millions of covenant women [and men]—from the beginning of time down through each and every gospel dispensation."[5]

I knew this man could not give me what I wanted in the eternal sense. I felt the flaxen cords begin to unwind from my soul. I knew I was a daughter of God—steadfast and immovable in keeping the commandments of God. The deep roots of my covenants that bound me to my Father in Heaven gave me the strength to flatly respond, "No."

I repeated my negative answer, and this time as I firmly said no, I was able to completely walk away from that relationship without looking back. I recognized that although I might have temporarily wanted the idea of love he presented, what I desired above all else were the promises from my Father in Heaven. I reminded myself once again: I knew His promises were sure.

That moment I said "no" and walked away from the unhealthy situation was a turning point for me. That decision led to more joy and happiness in my life than I ever could have imagined. Eldred G. Smith encouraged, "When you have resisted a temptation until it no longer becomes a temptation, then to that extent, Satan has lost his power over you, and as long as you do not yield to him, to that degree he is bound . . . then step by step; you may bind Satan now, you don't have to wait until the millennial reign."[6]

I still remember moving through the steps of repentance, but the thought of the concessions I had made no longer hurt or caused me sorrow. In my mind, I often see a portrait of myself saying, "No." Such a defining moment in my life! I had seen through the deceptions of Satan and had set aside *my* will for the will of the Lord.

The Joy of Repentance

I realized my view of reality in that situation had become distorted, focused on one exclusive goal—happiness. The truth is *all* of us who have experienced divorce are particularly susceptible to such a distortion because *any* circumstance is likely better than what we experienced in an extremely unhappy marriage.

Satan convinces us that the fleeting happiness or pleasure we may feel in a weak moment is all we need. Suppose we settle for that momentary pleasure versus the full happiness that Heavenly Father offers. In that case, we may become convinced that what we have is better than anything our Father in Heaven has promised or prepared for us.

However, if we make this mistake, we will miss the lasting joy and peace only found through our Savior. Neal A. Maxwell counseled, "Only by aligning our wills with God's is full happiness to be found. Anything less results in a lesser portion. The Lord will work with us even if, at first, we 'can no more than desire' but are willing to 'give place for a portion of [His] words.' A small foothold is all He needs! But we must desire and provide it."[7]

The battle to have faith in the unknown and rely on the promises of our Father in Heaven and our elder brother, Jesus Christ, is familiar to each of us. If the veil were withdrawn and we could see our pre-earth life, we would remember that our Father presented a plan to us that required a huge leap of faith.

We understood there would be dangers and temptations, but not all of us were willing to accept or trust the Father's plan. One-third of our brothers and sisters chose the easier, softer way that prohibited them from coming to the earth. They chose not to receive bodies. They chose not to grow, mature, or receive eternal salvation.

Heavenly Father values and honors our agency—our ability to choose. He will never force us to choose Him or His Son. He allows us to determine our own course through our actions and choices each day. So often we choose, like Esau, the "mess of pottage" over the birthright we have been promised.

Usually, we are unwilling to wait and trust in the Lord and His promises. We confuse fleeting happiness for eternal joy. Elder Scott taught, "Because he respects your agency, Father in Heaven will never force you to pray to Him. But as you exercise that agency and include Him in every aspect of your daily life, your heart will begin to fill with peace, buoyant peace. That peace will focus an eternal light on your struggles. It will help you to manage those challenges from an eternal perspective."[8]

Did you know repentance and joy go hand in hand? I did not, until this experience. When I was younger, I thought of repentance as a punishment for doing something wrong. One of my earliest memories was from when I was about four or five years old. I took a pack of gum from a small convenience store one day while shopping with my mother. I knew if I asked, she would not buy it for me, so I waited until she was busy purchasing the items she had selected. Then I carefully slipped the pack of gum in my pocket.

Once we got home, I ran to my room and pulled out the illicit pack, marveling that my theft had gone unsuspected. I felt a mild twinge of guilt for taking something that was not mine but happily distracted myself by unwrapping a piece of the gum and hastily putting it in my mouth. Then I went to play.

A couple hours later, my mother called me for dinner. I didn't want to throw out the precious piece of gum, so I stuck it right on the side of my plate, in plain view. My mother asked where I had gotten my gum. Wide-eyed, I shrugged my shoulders and replied, "I don't remember." My mother wisely did not ask anything more.

That night as I crawled into bed and my mother knelt beside me to help me say my prayers, I remember whispering that I didn't feel like praying. As the day had worn on, the guilt of what I had done began to weigh on my little mind, and I felt that God would not want to hear from me. My mother gently inquired why I didn't want to pray. In my shame, I whispered back, "I can't tell you." Instead, I pointed to my crumpled up jeans on the floor where I had left the remaining pack of gum in my pocket.

My mother picked up my jeans and searched my pockets, easily finding my offense. She immediately knew what I had done. I waited, holding my breath for the scolding. But it didn't come. Instead, my mother knelt beside me and asked me what I was feeling. I could only reply, "Bad. I feel bad."

Then she taught me a simple lesson on repentance. I understood I would have to take the pack of gum back to the store and talk to the owner, apologize for what I had done, and pay for the stolen gum. I don't remember many more details except I had to do some chores the next day around the house to earn money to pay for the gum.

Although some of the memories concerning that incident are hazy in my mind, I do know my mother did a wonderful job teaching me some of my first lessons of repentance. However, in my young mind, I twisted the lesson my mother had lovingly tried to teach into "repentance is a punishment for doing something wrong."

Furthermore, doing something "wrong" produced feelings of guilt and shame. I did not like feeling guilty or shameful and resolved to do my best to avoid feeling that way ever again. From that time on, I observed and analyzed people in my life and watched what they did "wrong." Then, I would try to make all correct choices, learning from their "mistakes." This method worked for a little while but eventually, being human, I would make a mistake and need to repent.

As I grew older, my understanding of repentance changed. During this season in my life, I would try to ignore my mistakes for as long as possible. Then, when the guilt of what I had done was a weight too heavy to bear, I would repent of all of my sins/wrongs in one fell swoop, and the process would start all over again. Such early repentance methods were torture and certainly not how our Savior intended for us to use His precious gift.

As an adult, I continued to repent out of duty because I had a keen sense of what was required to become a true disciple of Jesus Christ but felt little joy in the experience. It was not until I had the experience of walking away from that unhealthy relationship that my immature perceptions of repentance started to change. In Sunday School, a friend shared a thought that continued to increase my understanding of the principle of repentance. Sylvia explained that she knew she could not be perfect in this life, but she *could* be perfectly repentant. This concept was life-changing!

I began to view repentance as a gift—one that could bring me incomparable joy and peace. Elder Christofferson explains this principle as follows: "Repentance is a divine gift, and there should be a smile on our faces when we speak of it. Rather than interrupting the celebration, the gift of repentance is the cause for true celebration."[9] President Russell M. Nelson added, "When we choose to repent . . . we choose to receive joy—the joy of redemption."[10] Isn't that a beautiful promise? When we repent, we are promised joy, the "joy of redemption."

Consistently studying the Book of Mormon and especially the account of Alma the Younger continued the catalyst for shifting my mindset surrounding repentance. Alma's words to his son as he shared his conversion experience mirrored my own repentance experience: "I cried within my heart: O Jesus, thou Son of God, have mercy on me. . . . And behold, when I thought this, I could remember my pains no more; yea I was harrowed up by the memory of my sins no more. And oh, what joy, and what marvelous light I did behold, yea, my soul was filled with joy as exceeding as my pain!"[11]

Through Alma's account, we learn we are redeemed through the blood of Jesus Christ. Because of the Savior's sacrifice, we no longer have to bear the weight of our mistakes through the gift of repentance. Consequences still result from our actions, but we can feel joy simultaneously while repenting. Each of us needs repentance daily, or as I call them now, these "course corrections" can then become something we look forward to with eagerness, an ability to start fresh and try again.

The more I studied about repentance, the more I saw a connection between true repentance and joy. Alma references the word *joy* frequently in his account to his son. Often the scriptures use joy and happiness interchangeably. Yet, I learned there is a distinct difference between joy and worldly happiness.

Kevin J. Worthen describes joy with these three traits:

1. In its fulness, joy is a condition or state of being; it is a constant.
2. It comes from living in harmony with God's laws, from keeping His commandments.
3. We may not experience it fully in this life. Indeed, because of the limits of our mortal bodies and finite minds, we likely cannot even fully describe or understand this condition.

President Nelson noted, God "offers an intensity, depth, and breadth of joy that defy human logic or mortal comprehension." The scriptures indicate that we can completely experience "a fulness of joy" only after the resurrection when our perfected bodies and spirits are "inseparably connected."[12]

Joy is long-lasting; it comes as a result of our willingness to set aside what we want in the moment for what our Heavenly Father desires for us long-term. Joy is peace and "full happiness" combined. It is faith and trust in God's eternal plan for us. Joy comes as a result of keeping our covenants despite difficult circumstances and choosing to repent. Joy is found only in and through the love of Christ and the validation of our Heavenly Father.

Joseph Smith said joy or "happiness is the object and design of our existence."[13] If joy is the ultimate purpose of our being here on earth, doesn't that idea change how you view repentance? "Men [and women] are, that they might have joy!"[14]

We are meant to experience joy in this life in every facet of our lives—through trials, heartache, and joy in repentance. By the sacrifices of our beloved Savior, Jesus Christ, He becomes our advocate, thus enabling our peace and joy throughout our entire mortal experience. Kevin J. Worthen promises:

> When the focus of our lives is on God's plan of salvation . . . and Jesus Christ and His gospel, we can feel joy regardless of what is happening—or not happening—in our lives. Joy comes from, and because of Him. He is the source of all joy. For Latter-day Saints, Jesus Christ is joy! Thus, Christ is not only "the author and finisher of our faith" but is, in one sense, the author and finisher of our joy.

> We begin to have joy when we focus on Christ. We can then bring the power of Christ into our lives by focusing on joy.[15]

Language of the Spirit

Another essential lesson that helped further inoculate me against Satan's deception during this short but intense teaching season in my life came through an experience my sister shared with me one night. Summer was upon us, and we had an exceptionally clear sky. The two of us lay on the trampoline in my backyard. We gazed up at the stars and talked openly about life experiences and sacred moments.

My sister shared that she had received inspiration through the years in the form of dreams that had come to her. These dreams differed from her regular nighttime dreams, and they seemed to carry deep spiritual meaning for her as they came at turning points in her life. Her dreams made sense to her and helped her to know what she needed to do during difficult times.

As I listened to her experiences, I asked myself, how does God speak to me? How does He answer *my* prayers? I reflected on Elder Rasband's words, "The Spirit most often communicates as a feeling. You feel it in words that are familiar to you, that make sense to you."[16]

With Elder Rasband's encouragement, I dove into the scriptures with a renewed focus searching for answers. What I learned was invigorating! I read in the scriptures many things about how the Holy Spirit sounds, how He works, and His role in our lives. As I continued to study, concentrating especially on verses pertaining to the Holy Ghost, I began to have a clearer understanding of how God speaks to me.

My answers to prayers came into my heart and mind in the form of words while praying. To receive this inspiration, I needed to consistently immerse myself in the scriptures and pray daily. During my prayers, as I asked questions in faith, I trusted in the goodness of my Father in Heaven. I would sit still with a pen and paper in hand, listening for a reply. Then as words flowed into my mind, I would write the words and phrases down. Once I had recorded a prayer, I would express another prayer of gratitude. Then, I would *act* on the answers received in faith.

This method of receiving answers is very similar to what I shared in chapter 3. The main difference for me was some additional instruction I received while studying the scriptures that helped me discern the difference from my own thoughts and the voice of the Holy Ghost.

These are the general guidelines I discovered through study, to discern if the prompting comes from God:

1. What I am feeling agrees with scripture.
2. The message I am hearing is repeated.
3. The thought comes during prayer.
4. The prompting grows stronger with time.
5. What I am asked to do involves an element of faith.
6. The inspiration I am feeling invites me to do good.

As I look back over my experiences following my divorce, I can see that the answers I received followed the guidelines listed above. My job was to act in faith in response to the directions I had received. Most of the time, my directions were easier said than done. I required "acting in faith" practice.

Frequently, my pathway forward was not clear. I wanted to know where I was going and how I was going to get there. The Lord, however, gave me just enough information to take one step forward. I often had to wait and be patient. Listening and praying for the next piece of inspiration, I was led line upon line.

I used to ask myself why Heavenly Father didn't show us everything at once. The easy answer is that we would not be acting in faith, but I believe the Lord's motivation for not showing us everything at once is more than that. I have come to believe that our Father in Heaven does not show us everything all at once out of love for us. He shows us only enough so we can keep moving closer to Him if we choose. How might His strategy be an act of love?

Consider the example of a baby learning to walk: Parents simply focus on helping them first learn to crawl and then stand.

Next, the baby learns to use furniture as an aid. Through enough practice, the baby takes that first little wobbly step. As parents, we are so excited! We praise and encourage. Soon more steps follow. Sometimes we go a short distance away and encourage our little one to walk to us. We coax, call, and praise every step of the way until the child reaches its destination—our wide-open arms for a huge, loving hug.

Imagine for a moment that you are the parent of this child who is learning to walk. What if you see that first step and tell your baby, "Charlie, I am so excited! Look at this. You're going to walk to the couch and then go down the hallway, and then, at some point, you'll be tall enough to use this bathroom all by yourself."

Your baby would have no comprehension of your words. If he somehow did, he would feel completely overwhelmed and not understand all the directions nor the growth needed to reach the ultimate point. Wise parents simply encourage and praise those first few steps, and know in their hearts that they are witnessing the beginning of their child's journey down their path.

If Heavenly Father had prematurely shown me my life several years down the road, I would not have believed it. I could not have comprehended it, and part of me would have rejected that it could even be possible. Our Father in Heaven, in His wisdom, requires His children to walk by faith—a faith that strengthens us and helps us grow into the best version of ourselves. "For we walk by faith, not by sight."[17]

Time and practice are required to hear the voice of the Spirit. There is a great family home evening lesson on ChurchofJesusChrist.org that explains how learning to hear the voice of the Holy Ghost is similar to tuning an old radio.[18] To listen to the music you want, you have to turn a dial. As you turn the knob, it moves through the different stations.

Some stations have static and little to no sound. Some are blasting profane music, others political diatribes. You might stop at a station or two that hold your interest with a familiar or favorite song. We can become easily distracted by what sounds good on our way to what we truly want. James E. Faust warns, "The adversary tries to smother [us] with a multitude of loud, persistent, persuasive, and appealing voices. These voices will lead us away from the joy of the gospel. We must 'filter out' the static generated by Satan."[19]

Sometimes I have received a prompting that comes again and again into my mind. When I am unsure if it is from the Lord, I have learned that I should ask if it is from Him. Any time I have asked the Lord directly, I have been given a direct answer. Thus, I am able to distinguish a spiritual prompting from the noise and static generated by the adversary.

I once felt as though I would receive a certain church calling. The impression would not leave my mind. As I spoke with particular sisters, I would have the thought that she would make a great counselor/teacher/leader. At first, I prayed to have the thoughts leave my mind, but they became more persistent.

No matter what I did, the impression stayed in the back of my mind and began to color my thoughts and decisions. Finally, wanting to be free of it, I asked the Lord outright if these promptings were from Him. His response was no. I knew then that Satan was putting these thoughts into my head to distract me from what I needed to focus on in my current calling.

I realize that people often receive revelation about true future callings, and I don't doubt those accounts. I simply want to demonstrate that Satan will use any means to distract us from what we need to be doing. We must understand that through small means that may appear righteous, the adversary will attempt to thwart us.

However, Russell M. Nelson reassures:

> Imagine the miracle of it! . . . We can pray to our Heavenly Father and receive guidance and direction, be warned about dangers and distractions, and be enabled to accomplish things we simply could not do on our own. If we will truly receive the Holy Ghost and learn to discern and understand His promptings, we will be guided in matters large and small.[20]

Our best insurance for hearing the voice of the Spirit is to do everything we can to invite His guidance. I am able to hear the quiet promptings of the Holy Ghost more readily when I am consistently praying, studying my scriptures, attending the temple, and actively repenting. Then, I try to follow the promptings by acting in faith.

I have learned that if I am unsure about a prompting, I should ask! The Lord will not lead His children astray. Russell M. Nelson encourages us, "Choose to do the spiritual work required to enjoy the gift of the Holy Ghost and hear the voice of the Spirit more frequently and clearly."[21]

Remember my analogy of the gospel as a ladder to climb ever upward to heaven? Perhaps you have seen a similar metaphor in Sunday School, complete with a chalkboard illustration of a ladder with rungs labeled "baptism, temple covenants, mission, and temple marriage." A verse from the Bible often accompanies this type of lesson: "Enter ye in at the strait gate: for wide is the gate, and broad is the way, that leadeth to destruction, and many there be which go in thereat: Because strait is the gate and narrow is the way, which leadeth unto life, and few there be that find it."[22]

As I came to better understand the joy of repentance and tuned my heart to the whisperings of the Holy Ghost, I realized that my ladder analogy was false. My unintended interpretation of this scripture, meaning that the path is narrow and straight with our covenants and deeds as rungs of a ladder, made it especially hard when I no longer fit the "ideal" within the Church. This very scripture states that the way home to our Father in Heaven is, in fact, not a ladder but a straight and narrow path!

Following the Savior and relying on His grace is the only way we are able to return home to our Father in Heaven. Once we understand the Savior is the only way, then indeed, "strait is the gate, and narrow is the way." He is the way. There is no other way. "I have told you this that ye may learn wisdom, that ye may learn of me that there is no other way or means whereby man can be saved, only in and through Christ. Behold he is the life and the light of the world. Behold, he is the word of truth and righteousness."[23]

The adversary is a master at distorting gospel truths until they seem impossible to follow. Satan would have us believe that the path leading home to our Father in Heaven is so straight and narrow that we have no room for error. However, our covenant path home leaves room for repentance. It leaves room for errors. It allows for grace and mercy. There is no ladder to climb, no rungs to be knocked down from.

Our pathway home is following the Savior's example and tuning our hearts to the whisperings of the Spirit. Our journey will more than likely look like a meandering trail that twists back on itself from time to time. But our path forward is progress, not perfection. What matters is the direction we are going, and the intention of our actions. The path to our Father in Heaven is about who we are becoming, not just the list of what we are doing.

"God knows that you are not perfect, that you will fail at times. God loves you no less when you struggle than when you triumph. Like a loving parent, He merely wants you to keep intentionally trying. Discipleship is like learning to play the piano. Perhaps all you can do at first is play a barely recognizable rendition of "Chopsticks." But if you continue practicing, the simple tunes will one day give way to wondrous sonatas, rhapsodies, and concertos. Now, that day may not come during this life, but it will come. All God asks is that you consciously keep striving." [24]

—Dieter F. Uchtdorf

Lessons Learned: Chapter 6

1. The adversary knows who you are and seeks to destroy and limit your potential.
2. In moments where you feel tempted to go down a path that will not lead to eternal happiness, cling to the promises of the Lord. His promises are sure.
3. Reality can become distorted if we only look through the lens of our need to find happiness. Avoid confusing fleeting happiness for eternal joy.
4. Repentance is a gift that brings incomparable joy and peace.
5. Joy is faith and trust in God's eternal plan for us. It comes as a result of keeping our covenants.
6. Faith in a loving Father in Heaven strengthens us and helps us to grow into our best selves.
7. We are meant to experience joy in this life in every facet of our lives—through trials, heartache, and repentance.
8. It takes time and practice to hear the voice of the Holy Ghost.
9. Become an expert on how the Lord speaks to you through the Spirit. Do what is necessary to be worthy to receive continual revelation.
10. Our covenant path home leaves room for repentance; it leaves room for errors. It allows for grace and mercy.

"They were firm and steadfast, and immovable, willing with all diligence to keep the commandments of the Lord."[25]

Chapter 7

Partnering with Jesus Christ

"Salvation comes from partnering with Jesus Christ, from understanding His Atonement and His feelings of love from the women [and men] of the church." [1]

—Linda K. Burton

Personal Revelation

The trial of my divorce provided me an opportunity for advanced personal growth and a new understanding of many gospel principles. Enough time had passed that I began to see some of the fruits of my labors that were a result of my slow but deep changes. I was experiencing more peace and joy in my personal life, and, for the first time, I was not afraid of the future. However, as a single mom, the weight of running a household, working full-time, and raising my sons alone was, at times, overwhelming.

I took my children to every doctor, dentist, and orthodontist appointment. I filled and picked up monthly prescriptions. I attended every teacher meeting and school activity. My two younger sons were also in softball, so I drove them to and from practices and attended every game. My oldest was in the church youth program, so once a week, I dropped him off and picked up for his activities and made sure he had the opportunity to attend every dance or social opportunity. During this season of our lives, he attended a private school (on scholarship), which helped provide support for some of his special learning needs but required driving him to his school thirty minutes away from home and picking him up each afternoon. Sometimes the requirements of "mom duty" were staggering.

Most days, the moment I sat down for any length of time, I fell asleep out of sheer exhaustion. When I look back on the memory of that time, I cannot fathom how I physically and mentally did all that was required. I learned from Julie B. Beck that "because personal revelation is a constantly renewable source of strength, it is possible to feel bathed in help even during turbulent times."[2]

I can testify that I experienced this renewable source of strength daily, despite all the responsibilities and fatigue. I seemed to have the ability to do what was necessary, and I found myself experiencing moments of real joy and peace. I was happy. My sons were flourishing, and we were growing as a family unit, adjusting to our new life.

People often have misconceptions and confusion about the process of receiving revelation. They are wise to question: How do I know this is from God? How do I know if I'm hearing the voice of the Spirit? What if I make a mistake and I am deceived? I'm receiving a prompting that seems impossible; can it be right? These types of questions and more frequently come up in discussions about the subject of personal revelation.

As discussed previously, the first step in receiving answers to prayers is to be in tune with the Spirit and be worthy to receive communication from Him. The second step is to gather as much information as we can before we go before the Lord.

Oftentimes, we are unable to discern between choices because we lack enough information to make a decision. President Nelson instructs, "Personal revelation is based upon good information."[3] Sometimes, after a particular trial (like a divorce), we may have trouble trusting our own judgment. Past poor decisions may lead us to distrust ourselves. However, professional counselors, bishops, and trusted family members can help us navigate some of those issues.

Any time I have personally failed to trust my own judgment, it is because I want to be told what I should do to avoid accountability and eliminate any risk of getting it "wrong." Or I have resisted making any decision at all for fear I will make the wrong choice, allowing myself to sit on the proverbial fence, caught in indecision. None of these examples are conducive to receiving personal revelation. Julie B. Beck teaches, "The ability to qualify for, receive and act on personal revelation is the single most important skill that can be acquired in this life."[4]

Thankfully, for the most part, Heavenly Father has blessed us with sound minds. We have the ability to collect, gather, and store information. "For God hath not given us the spirit of fear; but of power, and of love, and of a sound mind."[5] We can reason things out in our minds, make a choice, and then pray to know if it is right. Then we act. If it is not the right choice, our Father in Heaven will not let us go down the road too long before helping us turn around (especially as we strive to stay close to the Spirit).

One of my favorite examples of Father in Heaven redirecting His earnestly seeking children to not go too far down the wrong path comes from a conference talk given a few years ago.

Jeffrey R. Holland and his son were driving down a stretch of road. When they came to an unfamiliar fork in the road, they prayed to know which direction to go and felt prompted to turn left. They drove about ten minutes down the road and came to a dead end. It had clearly been the wrong road. They turned around and took the other road when they got to the same junction. This road was long and windy. It did not seem correct, but they both knew it was right because they had already been down the wrong road. Despite the difficult circumstances, they were able to arrive at their destination safely. They felt that the Lord had blessed them by allowing them to travel down the wrong road first, making it a clear decision which was the right way.[6]

When we sincerely seek the Spirit and try our best to make good choices, Heavenly Father will help us make sure we arrive at our correct destination, even if it takes a little longer than we would have liked.

In addition to providing answers in which direction we should go, personal revelation can also protect us from literal attacks of the adversary. Before my divorce, while my then-husband and I were separated, our children were put in a life-threatening situation. I tried everything within my power as a mother to remove them from it, even going so far as to involve my bishop, elders quorum president, and even the police, all to no avail. I then had to rely solely on prayer and trust that my personal obedience to my covenants would protect my children.

The situation came to a head with much worse consequences than anyone could have imagined, but my sons were safe and protected. Afterward, I met with my bishop to discuss the events. He remarked that he had never seen a situation quite like what we had experienced, and it was clear an unseen power had preserved my sons. I believe my sons were protected by ministering angels because I was doing my best to honor and keep my covenants. Sister Bingham taught, "[Having access to priesthood power] means that we can receive revelation, be blessed and aided by the ministering of angels, learn to part the veil separates us from our Heavenly Father, be strengthened to resist temptation, be protected, and be enlightened."[7]

This experience strengthened my testimony that even when circumstances are out of our control, the Lord is always in charge. When we honor our covenants, we are entitled to receive revelation and added protection for ourselves and those within our stewardship. Since that experience, I have asked for ministering angels to attend my sons on multiple occasions. As a daughter of God and a covenant-keeping woman, I have the privilege of asking for those blessings on behalf of my children with the confidence that the Lord will honor my request. I have come to depend literally on the promises found in the scriptures. "For he will fulfill all his promises which he shall make unto you, for he has fulfilled his promises which he has made unto his fathers."[8]

Personal revelation became an essential lifeline to navigate the arduous waters of my life. I could not get through a single day without falling to my knees and pouring out my heart to my Father in Heaven. I felt gratitude for all the miracles I had experienced and the strength I had received to endure my trials.

As I prayed for answers, I found that they would often come through friends or those ministering to me. I relied on President Nelson's counsel concerning revelation: "Pour out your heart to your Heavenly Father. Turn to Him for answers and for comfort. Pray in the name of Jesus Christ about your concerns, your fears, your weaknesses—yes, the very longings of your heart. And then listen! Write the thoughts that come to your mind. Record your feelings and follow through with actions that you are prompted to take. As you repeat this process day after day, month after month, year after year, you will grow into the principle of revelation."[9] The answers I sought did not always come immediately, but with time and patience, the answers came.

Covenant-Belonging

An increase in personal revelation in my life led to a better understanding of covenant-belonging and the role it played in my life. Covenant-belonging is a result of righteous living and daily personal revelation. When we make and keep covenants with our Father in Heaven, we become covenant keepers.

As we keep our covenants and experience daily personal revelation through righteous living, we experience covenant-belonging. Elder Gong teaches:

> The age-old paradox is still true. In losing our worldly self through covenant belonging, we find and become our best eternal self—free, alive, real—and define our most important relationships. Covenant belonging is to make and keep solemn promises to God and each other through sacred ordinances that invite the power of godliness to be manifest in our lives. When we covenant all we are, we can become more than we are. Covenant belonging gives us place, narrative, capacity to become. It produces faith unto life and salvation.[10]

For a long time, when I would hear the word *covenant*, I would automatically think of the temple ordinances. But when we are baptized, we also make sacred covenants. We promise to take upon us the Savior's name and to always remember Him. Sister Burton instructed, "Making and keeping covenants means choosing to bind ourselves to our Father in Heaven and Jesus Christ. It is committing to follow the Savior. It is trusting in Him and desiring to show our gratitude for the price he paid to set us free through the infinite gift of the Atonement."[11]

I have always liked the similitude of taking Christ's name just as a wife takes a husband's last name. I appreciated this metaphor even more so after my divorce. To me, taking the Savior's name upon myself meant that I would be known as a disciple of Christ. I would be marked as His and bound to Him. As I came to better understand the principle of covenant-belonging, I began to recognize a pattern repeated over and over in the lives of covenant-belonging individuals found in the scriptures. I'll share the pattern first through scripture and then in my own life as I strived to practice covenant-belonging.

The Book of Mormon opens with a great example of covenant-belonging in action. Nephi was taught line upon line to first become a covenant keeper, which then led him to experience covenant-belonging in his day to day life.

Here is the pattern of covenant-belonging:

1. Having faith in Jesus Christ (which leads us to make covenants).
2. Believing in the promises of a loving Father in Heaven.
3. Acting in obedience to the promptings and revelation we receive.
4. Relying wholly on the Lord.
5. Patiently enduring and trusting in the Lord's timing.

Nephi was born to good parents who taught him and his siblings gospel truths. Nephi's father, Lehi, was a prophet and warned the wicked people of Jerusalem that they would be destroyed unless they repent. The people mocked and scorned him. Later, Lehi had a vision and shared it with his family. In the vision, Lehi was told to flee Jerusalem with his family because people wanted to kill him. Nephi was obedient and supported his father in preparing the family to leave immediately. He believed in his father's vision.

Once they left Jerusalem and were living in the wilderness in a tent, Nephi realized he needed to have his own testimony to be able to do all that the Lord required of their family. He went up into a mountain and prayed to have his own witness that what his father had seen and testified is true. "Wherefore I did cry unto the Lord and behold he did visit me and did soften my heart that I did believe all the words which had been spoken of by my father. And it came to pass that the Lord spake unto me, saying: Blessed are thou, Nephi, because of thy faith, for thou hast sought me diligently, with lowliness of heart. And inasmuch as ye shall keep my commandments, ye shall prosper."[12]

The Lord answered Nephi's inquiries of faith by showing him the same vision his father had. He also promised Nephi that as he was faithful, he would prosper. Nephi trusted the promises of the Lord and had faith that as he was obedient, those promises would be his.

Later, Lehi shared the revelation with his sons that they had been commanded to go back to Jerusalem and retrieve brass plates from Laban. Nephi's reply to his father's entreaty is a well-known scripture and exemplifies his testimony and the confidence he has in the Lord's promises. He stated, "I will go do the things which the Lord hath commanded, for I know that the Lord giveth no commandments unto the children of men, save he shall prepare a way for them that they may accomplish the thing which he commandeth them."[13]

When I was younger, I thought that Nephi was overly confident in stating that he *knew*. I wanted to ask, "How does he know?" I understand this better now, looking at it through the lens of Nephi becoming a covenant-belonging individual.

What the Lord was asking of Lehi's sons was not easy, and there was no guarantee that everyone would come back alive. But Nephi was able to have faith and confidence in the Lord because he was obeying the commandments and experiencing personal revelation. These foundational elements of covenant-belonging enabled Nephi to have the faith necessary to do what he was asked.

Those familiar with the story know that Nephi and his brothers were obedient and returned to Jerusalem. They were initially unsuccessful in retrieving the plates multiple times and almost lost their lives in their efforts. Nephi's older brothers, Laman and Lemuel, got angry and turned on Nephi. They beat him and even tried to kill him, but an angel of the Lord intervened and stopped them.

At any point during this whole experience, Nephi could have said, "Lord, I tried. In fact, I've tried really hard. I'm being obedient, I have faith, and I am relying on you, but I am just not seeing the fulfillment of all that you promised. I quit." However, Nephi did not quit. Instead, when things were difficult, Nephi had even greater faith and reliance on the Lord.

He forgave his brothers and prepared to try again to retrieve the plates. While Laman and Lemuel were ready to go back to their father in the wilderness empty-handed, Nephi was not willing to accept defeat. He admonished his brothers to remember all that the Lord had done for them. Then, Nephi went forward in faith, stating, "And I was led by the Spirit, not knowing beforehand the things which I should do."[14]

Nephi was successful in retrieving the plates through a series of events that can only be described as miraculous. He joyfully returned with the plates to his father and mother in the wilderness. The realization of what he was commanded to do led to an increase in Nephi's willingness to be exactly obedient to all the Lord asks of him. Nephi was seeing the hand of the Lord at work in his life. His willingness to be exactly obedient was a fruition of covenant-belonging.

After all the trials Nephi experienced, the reader might think: Now Nephi has earned a moment to pause and rejoice! However, Nephi was asked to immediately return to Jerusalem a second time. This time he and his brothers were directed to bring another family with them into the wilderness so that Nephi and his brothers can marry. (I like to think the Lord required this second trip for many reasons, but one of them was to give Laman and Lemuel another chance. The Lord's arm of mercy is *always* extended for us!) This mission was also successful.

Fast forward eight years. Nephi and his family were still in the wilderness. He and his father had amazing visions and testimony-building experiences. Nephi had married a righteous woman and had apparently become a father himself. He testified, "And it came to pass that we did again take our journey in the wilderness, and we did travel and wade through much affliction in the wilderness, and our women did bear children in the wilderness. And so great were the blessings of the Lord upon us, our women . . . were strong, yea, even like unto the men; and they began to bear their journeyings without murmuring."[15]

I love this perspective because it shows that not only had Nephi continued being faithful to the Lord's commandments, but through their trials, Nephi's family learned to rely wholly on the Lord and express gratitude for all that they have been blessed with. They had become a covenant-belonging people and were witnessing the power of godliness in their daily lives.

In our modern-day society, Satan tries to convince us that if we are doing all the right things, life should feel easier, look better, and not require as much effort from us. But that is simply not true. Joseph Smith taught, "Let us here observe that a religion that does not require the sacrifice of all things never has power sufficient to produce the faith necessary unto life and salvation."[16]

Life continued to be difficult for Nephi and his family. They experienced deaths, tribulations, trials, and wars. But, thirty years after they had left Jerusalem, despite all they had suffered, Nephi states with joy, "And it came to pass that we lived after the manner of happiness."[17]

Joy amidst tribulation is the promise of covenant-belonging.

Following the example found in the scriptures and looking for the same pattern, I witnessed firsthand the power of covenant-belonging working in my own life. After my divorce, my sons and I lived on substantially less income than we had before. I received multiple priesthood blessings over the years, reassuring me that Heavenly Father was personally acquainted with my needs and those of my family.

I was promised that we would always have enough food to eat and that all our essentials would be taken care of. This promise was especially comforting to me, as I was self-employed. Due to the promises of those blessings, I had complete faith that our temporal and physical needs would be provided for. I just didn't always know how the Lord would accomplish this.

Unfortunately, a year and a half after my divorce, the income from my independent contracting job had trickled down to a very small amount—not enough to realistically live on. I didn't know where the money would come from to pay the bills and put food on our table. After much prayer, I knew it was time for me to look for regular employment.

This meant that I needed to find a job outside of my home for the first time in fifteen years. I hoped to find a position that would allow me to still care for my children's needs. Ideally, I was looking for a job in my field of training that allowed me to work the same hours that my children were in school. Finding a job that specific felt daunting, but I had faith in the promises I had been given.

I resolved to do all I could do to facilitate the miracle I needed. I created an updated resume and sent it out to a few people for feedback. Next, I made inquiries with well-connected friends and family members and sent them my new resume. Within twenty-four hours, I had several encouraging responses and was offered an interview for a job that dovetailed nicely with the field in which I had been self-employed.

I was extremely nervous about getting ready for the interview. I spent some time on my knees, talking to my Father in Heaven about my concerns. As I prepared to leave for the interview, I felt peace. I knew my family and I were in the hands of the Lord.

The interview went well, and I was offered the job on the spot. I was ecstatic! But, I still needed to broach the subject of my work hours coordinating with my children's school schedule. The owner listened carefully to my plea. Amazingly, he consented to the schedule I requested. His concession was a miracle to me.

All those seemingly impossible pieces all came together a mere forty-eight hours after I had prayerfully made the decision to get a new job! I felt this blessing was a direct result of my keeping and honoring my covenants. Like Nephi, I had been wholly reliant upon my Father in Heaven, not knowing beforehand the things that I should do. I moved forward in faith, doing all I could to prepare to receive the blessings the Lord had in store for my family and me.

My new job was such a blessing to our family. I earned exactly the right amount of income for us to pay our bills. Three months after starting the job, I was proficient enough to earn a monthly bonus on top of my regular pay each month. That bonus allowed me to put away a small amount each month for emergencies and continue paying off some debt from the divorce.

But, what if the promised blessings don't come as we expect? What if prayers seem to go unanswered? What if the righteous miracles we are pleading for do not come to fruition?

There have been many times in my life when I have not received the asked for miracles, and the answers to prayers do not come. Through my trials and learning to trust my Father in Heaven, I have gained a firm testimony that when prayers go unanswered, we must go back to that first step of covenant-belonging—faith.

Mustering faith can be hard when we do not (indeed cannot) know all the answers or understand all the reasons blessings are withheld, even temporarily. Thankfully, our Father in Heaven requires only a mustard seed-size of faith from us. With it, we are promised we can move mountains! Elder Renlund reassures, "If a desired blessing from God has not been received—yet—you do not need to go crazy, wondering what more you need to do. Instead, 'cheerfully do all things that lie in [your] power; and then stand still, with the utmost assurance, to see the arm [of God] revealed.' Some blessings are reserved for later, even for the most valiant of God's children."[18]

Paul comfortingly testifies of many men and women who received great blessings, but not immediately: "These all died in the faith, not having received the promises, but having seen them afar off."[19] Faith is trusting in God's word. It is believing in something not visible. Sometimes faith is about enduring. Sometimes the blessings of faith do not show up in this life, but through faith, we can obtain all that Father in Heaven has promised us. Trusting in His promises is an act of faith and is the foundation of covenant-belonging.

Nephi trusted the promises of the Lord and had faith that as he was obedient, those promises would be his. What is astounding is some of those promises did not come to him and his family until thirty years later! He continued faithfully moving forward, trusting they would come in the Lord's own time. As we are obedient to our covenants, those blessings are ours to claim, no matter how long they take to come.

Blessings of Obedience

"Obedience brings success; exact obedience brings miracles." [20]

—Russell M. Nelson

During this time, I experienced a happy change in my life and an answer to a prayer. At the close of the previous school year, the house I had been renting came under contract for purchase. I had been faithfully searching for months for a new rental home. I had very few requirements. My sons could share bedrooms, and we could share a single bathroom if necessary (though being the only female in the house, I preferred having my own). My biggest concern was finding a home within our budget. I had tried to find every way possible to make something, *anything,* work. The market for rentals was competitive, and it seemed that every time I found an available rental, it would be gone before I could even inquire.

After experiencing multiple let-downs, I reached a point in my search where there was nothing available within my budget. I called my mom to express my frustration. She listened sympathetically but encouraged me to look again immediately. I was a little taken aback that she insisted I look again, right then. I replied, somewhat annoyed, "Mom, I literally just looked, and there is nothing listed that's in our budget."

She responded, "Noelle, I understand. Can I encourage you to look one more time?"

I was silently resistant but obediently opened the app I had been using to search for rentals. Instantly I saw that a brand-new listing had come available for a home within our budget. I was astounded! After apologizing to my mother, I called the number.

The owners answered and fortuitously were currently at the house! They said that they would be happy to show it to me, so I got in my car and drove right over. This house was less than ten minutes away from our current rental but in a completely different area from where I had ever lived.

The home was situated in a cul-de-sac near an elementary school. When I pulled up to the address, I was honestly somewhat disappointed at the appearance of the outside of the house. It was a little weather-worn and in need of a fresh coat of paint. However, I took a deep breath and thought, "I have nothing to lose; I might as well go take a look."

The door was open, and I tapped gently on it to announce my arrival. The owner opened the door and welcomed me in. We stepped into a modest but clean and carpeted living room with a lovely brick façade and gas fireplace. From there, we moved into the kitchen, which I could tell had been completely redone. It had new countertops, tile flooring, and cupboards. The kitchen area opened into a spacious dining room, and off it was a cozy nook ideal for an office. Along the back wall, a door led to the backyard.

As we opened that door and stepped into the yard, we found a nice deck in good repair. The backyard itself had been cemented over, to my disappointment—no grass for my sons to play on. Then I noticed a gate along the back fence.

I pulled the string, and the gate swung open to what seemed to be acres and acres of green grass surrounding a massive playground. The house was situated right against the back of the elementary school. The gate opened directly to the playing fields of the school! My sons would literally be able to walk out the back door to get to school and just as easily walk home each day.

The rest of the house was amazingly ideal—hardwood floors, marble tile in all the bathrooms, a private bath off the master bedroom, a generous master closet, two more bedrooms, and a one-car garage.

I had never seen 1,300 square feet so perfectly proportioned and elegantly redone. Everything inside was beautiful and new. The home was owned by an older couple who had spent the last six months updating and refurbishing it. The only thing they had not done yet was repaint the outside of the house.

I fell in love with this little house. It was everything we needed and so much more. I had built a good rapport with the owners as I walked through the house, and I told them I would like to rent their home. I was honest about my situation—single mom, recently self-employed, at a new job, and working to repair her credit. The owners kindly listened and expressed that they felt I was the person who should rent their home despite the risks. In just an hour, I had found and signed papers for our new home. It was a miracle, and it was an even nicer home than the beautiful rental we would be leaving.

What was it about this little house and all the mundane rental details that made it so miraculous?

For me, it was a tangible manifestation of the Lord's desire to bless my family with even more than what I had asked. It also demonstrated the law of obedience in action within my life. Elder Renlund taught, "When you receive any blessing from God, you can conclude that you have complied with an eternal law governing reception of that blessing." He also instructed, "Blessings are neither earned by frenetically accruing 'good deed coupons' nor by helplessly waiting to see if we win the blessing lottery. Restored truth reveals that faith-inspired actions on our part, both initial and ongoing are essential."[21]

I had diligently been obeying the commandments and honoring my covenants. The more obedient I was, the more the Lord was able to bless me, and the more obedient I desired to be.

I realized that in the past, I had been obedient out of fear of making God mad. As I matured, I obeyed out of duty. Following my divorce, fear and duty were replaced with love as I became more acquainted with God's true nature through His Son, Jesus Christ. My increased obedience demonstrated through my actions an increase in love and trust in God. I relied on the promise found in Romans, "And we know that all things work together for good to them that love God, to them who are the called according to his purpose."[22]

As I continued to study the scriptures the phrase "observe to perform every word of command with exactness" caught hold in my mind. "Yea and they did obey and observe to perform every word of command with exactness; yea, and even according to their faith, it was done unto them."[23] I wrote the words "obey every word and command with exactness, out of love for my Savior" on a sticky note and taped it to my bathroom mirror. Each morning and night, I read those words and worked to obey every law and command out of my deep love for my Father in Heaven.

I had hoped and asked for a few of the necessities the house came with, but because I was willing to ask, act in faith, and prepare myself, Heavenly Father confirmed that I was worthy to receive those blessings, plus so much more. Finding that little house was nothing short of a miracle. I have a firm testimony that blessings follow obedience. The timing may be different from what we expect, but the Lord always fulfills His promises. President Nelson explained this principle best when he said, "All blessings are predicated by obedience to the law. . . . To every kingdom, there is a law given."[24] If we follow the laws of that kingdom, we can expect to be blessed.

As I reflected over the past months, I realized how far I had come personally and how far we had come as a family. I thought back to the many unhappy days and nights I had lived through in our old house. That house had been such a blessing at the time, but I looked forward to moving into this new home to begin a happier chapter with my children.

We immediately moved into that little house. Our home was filled with love, laughter, and happiness. Some of the greatest blessings of our lives came while we lived in that special place.

I was thrilled with the knowledge that the Lord was intimately aware of our family and all our needs, even those unspoken. I saw the miracle of finding our home a fruition of partnering with the Savior and a direct result of my obedience.

I reiterate the words of Nephi when he said, "Let us be faithful in keeping the commandments of the Lord, for behold he is mightier than all the earth."[25] The God we worship as covenant-belonging daughters and sons of God is the creator of the earth. He is mightier than all the earth! Covenant-belonging is a testament that we can experience joy when we choose to belong to the Lord despite great hardships. We are His, and He forgets not His own.

"Faith is the power; obedience is the price; love is the motive; the Spirit is the key, and Christ is the reason." [26]

—James E. Faust

Lessons Learned: Chapter 7

1. Personal revelation is a daily renewable source of strength.
2. To receive personal revelation requires us to first gather good information. This allows us to then be able to make a decision to take to the Lord to receive revelation for our lives.
3. Sometimes we must go down the wrong road for a bit to be able to turn around and trust more fully in the Savior.
4. When we honor our covenants, we are entitled to receive revelation and added protection for ourselves and those within our stewardship.
5. When we make and keep covenants with our Father in Heaven, we are covenant keepers. Then as we practice keeping our covenants and work to receive daily personal revelation, we can experience covenant belonging. Covenant belonging gives a "place, narrative, and the ability to become."
6. Joy amidst tribulation is a promise of covenant-belonging.
7. Sometimes the blessings of faith do not show up in this life, but through faith, we *can* obtain all that Father in Heaven has promised us.
8. Trusting in the Savior's promises is an act of faith and is the foundation of covenant-belonging.
9. Choose to obey every word and command with exactness, out of love for the Savior.
10. Blessings follow obedience. The timing may be different from what we expect, but the Lord always fulfills His promises.

"First, I obey, then I understand." [27]

—Marjorie Pay Hinckley

Chapter 8

Thy Faith Hath Made Thee Whole

"I testify that bad days will come to an end, that faith always triumphs, and that heavenly promises are always kept." [1]

—Jeffrey R. Holland

Tabernacle Made Temple

In the early morning hours of December 17, 2010, smoke began to billow out of the Provo Tabernacle in downtown Provo, Utah. Firefighters were quickly called in and began the arduous task of putting out the fire while protecting the city's beautiful and treasured landmark.

After several hours, all efforts to extinguish the fire were unsuccessful. The firefighters were instructed to retreat to preserve their lives, as the fire was simply too intense and could not be suppressed. Shortly after that, the heat from the flames blew out the windows. Then, the roof collapsed, much to the horror of the onlookers who had gathered outside. One witness interviewed by the media shared, "To see it [gone] tears my heart."[2]

It was gone. The tabernacle that had been central to the city of Provo for over one hundred years stood no longer. As the smoke ceased billowing and the flames finally died down, the extent of the damage was yet possible to assess.

The destruction to the tabernacle was severe, and it was unknown if there would be a way to repair the devastation the fire had caused. All that remained of the original structure were the four charred exterior brick walls. John Curtis, Mayor of Provo City, summed up the feelings of a city devastated by the recent destruction: "Many of us are going through something of a grieving process."[3] "This building . . . was . . . part of our fabric."[4]

The Provo City Tabernacle had served the area for more than a century. It was an edifice rich with history and replete with sweet memories for members of The Church of Jesus Christ of Latter-day Saints. It had been the site of past general conferences and even had entertained a visit in 190 9 from the United States President, Howard Taft. In more recent years, the chapel had held many musical concerts, housed stake and regional conferences, and had been central to numerous families' holiday traditions.

As the shock of loss wore off, the inevitable question of what would happen to the building arose. Discouragement amid questions ensued: Could any part of it be salvaged? What could be done to preserve the tabernacle's history?

The Church of Jesus Christ of Latter-day Saints, owners of the property, issued a statement reflecting their sorrow at losing such an important icon. But Church leaders provided not even a hint concerning any plans for the property. Spring and summer passed. Finally, in the October 2011 general conference, President Thomas S. Monson announced a formal plan for the Provo Tabernacle: "After careful study, we've decided to rebuild it. With full preservation and restoration of the exterior to become the second temple in the Church in the city of Provo."[5]

The announcement at the conference center that afternoon in downtown Salt Lake City sent shock waves of surprise and exclamations of joy throughout the congregation. There were tears at the choice to preserve this building and elevate it to one of the holiest houses that can be constructed on earth. The decision to rebuild the tabernacle spoke volumes that the prophet and leaders of the Church acknowledged its significance and did not consider it beyond restoration.

Reconstruction began shortly after the announcement that fall. The crew of men and women assigned to complete the task of reconstructing the tabernacle were asked to do something that had never been done before. They recognized that their first task was to strengthen the foundation, but in order to strengthen the foundation, they had to simultaneously protect and secure the fragile remnants of the upper brick walls.

The entire building was put on stilts to secure the walls. Originally constructed with five layers of brick, these walls had been so damaged by smoke and fire that only three rows of brick remained. However, the three rows were enough to preserve the unique design and footprint of the building. The original brick was then strengthened inside and layered with concrete to ensure its stability. The outer walls were essential to preserve and maintain the unique look of the building.

With the walls secured, architects turned their attention to the foundation. After extensive examination, they found that the foundation needed to go another forty feet below the water table. The foundation was waterproofed similarly to that of a boat or bathtub. This deeper foundation allowed space for two more basement floors to be added to the framework's original footprint, tripling the structure's actual size. Once the upper walls were secured and the foundation was in place, construction on the rest of the building commenced.

The building's history was considered in the design of every detail, from the grand staircases to the intricately patterned doorknobs. Even the exit signs were designed to look as if they belonged to the original nineteenth-century construction. An exquisite stained-glass image of the Savior was hung to greet all who walk through the front door. There were subtle arches added throughout the entire building echoing the original architect John Watkins's design style. The crowning achievement of the beautiful edifice was the gold-leafed Moroni statue placed atop the restored central tower of this newly built house of the Lord.

In March of 2016, the new Provo City Center Temple was officially dedicated. The work had taken five years, from preserving the original building's outer walls to the furnishing of the inside with thoughtful reminders of the structure's past history. As the newly dedicated Provo City Center Temple, the building had been taken far beyond its former glory and now dedicated in "holiness to the Lord."

Robert D. Hales expressed, "Each of us must go through certain experiences to become more like our Savior. In the school of mortality, the tutor is often pain and tribulation, but the lessons are designed to refine and bless and strengthen us, not destroy us."[6] The reconstruction of the tabernacle to a holy temple became a symbol of the rebuilding and restoring of my own personal life after my divorce.

Restored

The tabernacle and I, holy creations from the Lord.
Both tabernacles burnt—one by fire, the other by divorce.
I wonder at the ashes of my life—searching for the beauty.
Slowly and patiently the Savior shows me the woman I can become.

I sink my roots deeper into the gospel as my covenants bind me to Him.
At times I am overwhelmed by the sheer magnitude of the task before me—
How can I become this woman that only He sees?
Quietly the answers come—line upon line, one by one
I realize His work with me is not done.
I am strengthened beyond my former capacity,
Redeemed by love for something more.
We are one in the same, the tabernacle and I.
Houses dedicated to the Lord—
Renewed, redressed, and restored.

—NM

Process of Refinement

"Adversity should not be viewed as either disfavor from the Lord or a withdrawal of His blessings. Opposition in all things is part of a refiner's fire to prepare us for eternal destiny." [7]

—Quentin L. Cook

There was a time during my divorce and the ensuing months when I felt broken and defeated. My entire life, I had tried my best to choose to do the right thing. When I ended up a single mom, barely able to make ends meet, I became mired in discouragement with no prospect of a different future. I cried out to the Lord in my deep sorrow, asking what I had done to deserve any of this. I did not understand that the Lord saw so much more for my life than the small view I had in those moments.

To receive all the blessings the Lord had in store for me, I had to endure the refiner's fire. "That the trial of your faith, being much more precious than of gold that perisheth, though it be tried with fire, might be found unto praise and honour and glory at the appearing of Jesus Christ."[8] I found encouragement and further understanding for the process of refinement in the modern-day parable of the "Silversmith."

> One day, a group of women gathered for their weekly Bible study. On this particular day, they read verses in Malachi. "And he shall sit as a refiner and purifier of silver: and he shall purify the sons [and daughters] . . . , and purge them as gold and silver, that they may offer unto the Lord an offering in righteousness.'"
>
> This verse was puzzling to the group as they did not have any understanding of working with precious metals. One of the members offered to learn about the process of refining silver and inform them of her findings at their next study.
>
> She visited a silversmith and watched him work. As she watched, the silversmith held a silver piece over the fire and let it heat up. The silversmith explained that you must hold the silver directly in the middle of the fire, where the flames are hottest to burn away all the impurities in refining silver. The woman then thought about God holding us where the flames are the hottest to burn away our impurities.
>
> Then the woman recalled part of the verse. 'And he shall sit as a refiner and purifier of silver.' She asked the silversmith if it was true that he had to sit there in front of the fire and watch the process at all times. The silversmith answered that not only did he have to sit there holding the silver, but he had to keep his eyes on the silver the entire time it was tested in the fire. If the silver was left a moment too long in the flames, it would be destroyed.
>
> The silversmith further instructed: you must leave it long enough to serve the purpose, but not too long as it would destroy it. The member was silent for a moment. Then she asked the silversmith, 'How do you know when silver is fully refined?' The silversmith smiled and answered, 'Oh, that's easy — when I see my image in it.'
>
> When you feel the heat of the fire, remember that God has his eye on you, and He will 'sit as a refiner and purifier' keeping watch until He sees His image in you. God is intimately aware of your needs and limits. He also knows just when you have had enough. At the right time, He will remove you from the fire.[9]

My Father in Heaven allowed the trial of my divorce to burn off the impurities in my own life. He used my divorce as a tool to refine and perfect me. I am not referring to the traditional English definition of perfection, which is without a flaw, but to the Greek definition, which means wholly, completely, or thoroughly.

Isn't that a beautiful definition? The Greek definition changes the traditional scripture, "Be ye therefore perfect, even as your Father which is in heaven, is perfect,"[10] to instead read, "Be ye therefore whole, even as your Father which is in Heaven, is whole."

We came to earth knowing we would have trials—some of our own making, which would require repentance on our part. The Savior paid the price for our sins. We are taught, "But he was wounded for our transgressions; he was bruised for our iniquities: the chastisement of our peace was upon him, and with his stripes we are healed."[11] However, we also came to earth knowing that we would experience some tribulations, not of our own design. We would suffer consequences from other people's choices and experience heartbreaking circumstances that are a natural part of living in a fallen world.

We may wonder, are these trials, not of our origination also addressed in the Savior's infinite Atonement?

The answer is found in the phrase "the chastisement of our peace was upon him."[12] To chastise means to redress or restore. The situations that we did not cause would still require restoration. The Savior's sacrifice includes all issues that require redress. He paid the price so that we did not have to carry the weight and sorrow caused by someone else's choices. By His wounds, we are literally healed. That is the miracle!

Not only were our sins a part of the Savior's sacrifice, but all our suffering from any sickness, any injustices, all wrongs, and all our heartaches allow us to petition our Savior for restoration, for healing, for peace. We can become whole through His matchless sacrifice. Every part of our mortal experience in this life was thought of and planned for by a loving Father in Heaven who perfectly understood what His children would need, even before we could know. He sent His Son to live for us and to die for us.

> How could the Father tell the world of love and tenderness?
> He sent his Son, a newborn babe, with peace and holiness.

How could the Father show the world the pathway we should go?
He sent His Son to walk with men on earth that we may know.
How could the Father tell the world of sacrifice, of death?
He sent His Son to die for us and rise with living breath.
What does the Father ask of us? What do the scriptures say?
Have faith, have hope, live like his Son, help others on their way.
What does He ask? Live like his Son.[13]

We cannot be perfected or completed in this life without the grace of the Atonement of Jesus Christ. In other words, we cannot be *whole* in this life without the Savior Jesus Christ. The truth is we were never meant to suffer our hardships and trials alone.

God loves us completely, not in bits and pieces or partially, but perfectly, and wholly, without reservation. We are His children. Our Father in Heaven has done everything for us and has even prepared a way for the hardest, most painful things in our lives to be transformed into priceless treasures, opportunities for growth, and change.

The way has been perfectly prepared for us through His Son, Jesus Christ. Through the Atonement of our Savior, we can be succored, strengthened, and have our burdens made lighter. Elder Eyring reminds us, "The burdens His faithful servants must carry in life are made lighter by His Atonement."[14]

Yoking Ourselves to the Savior

I grew up in an age when The Oregon Trail computer game was part of history class in elementary school. I remember being chased by Native Americans, running out of food, contracting diphtheria, and having my oxen die—all before some of our party made it to our destination. When I hear the word yoke, I think of that pixelated computer image of two oxen sharing a wooden yoke, pulling a wagon to Oregon.

I have since learned that no progress can be made if one ox is pulling one way while the other pulls another. Both animals must trust the master and be united in pursuing their destination while pulling the load. The weight of the load is too great for just one ox, but the yoke helps to distribute the weight between the two oxen, allowing each to support the other and make progress.

The Savior entreats, "Come unto me, all ye that labor and are heavy laden, and I will give you rest. Take my yoke upon you, and learn of me; for I am meek and lowly in heart: and ye shall find rest unto your souls. For my yoke is easy, and my burden is light."[15]

Do we understand what it means to yoke ourselves to the Savior? To find rest for our souls and to have the burdens we must bear made lighter?

Yoking ourselves with the Savior means setting aside our will for our Heavenly Father's will; that is, "trusting the Master." It means believing in our Savior's grace and keeping sight of our eternal destination.

As we focus on who we are becoming versus what we are doing, we work with our Savior, His grace enabling us to do more than we can do alone. Elder Bednar promises, "We are not and never need be alone. We can press forward in our daily lives with heavenly help. Through the Savior's Atonement, we can receive capacity and 'strength beyond [our] own.'"[16]

There is no better example, found in the scriptures, of a people "yoking themselves to the Savior, and receiving a strength, not their own" than of Alma and his people, while they were subjects under the wicked Lamanite king, Amulon.

> For Amulon knew Alma, that he had been one of the king's priests, and that it was he that believed the words of Abinadi . . . and therefore he was wroth with him. . . . He exercised authority over them, and put tasks upon them, and put task-masters over them. And it came to pass that so great were their afflictions that they began to cry mightily to God. And Amulon commanded them that they should stop their cries; and he put guards over them to watch them, that whosoever should be found calling upon God should be put to death. And Alma and his people did not raise their voices to the Lord their God but did pour out their hearts to him, and he did know the thoughts of their hearts.[17]

I love these verses! Alma's people could not speak the words of their prayers aloud, but that did not stop them from speaking their prayers in their hearts and minds. With every fiber of their beings, they were seeking the Lord and praising Him. They exercised patience in their afflictions. The people of Alma trusted their Savior.

"And it came to pass that the voice of the Lord came to them in their afflictions, saying: Lift up your heads and be of good comfort, for I know of the covenant which ye have made unto me; and I will covenant with my people and deliver them out of bondage."[18]

When the Lord tells them to "be of good comfort," He is lovingly comforting them in their afflictions, as a parent would console a child through a difficult time. The Savior assures the people of Alma that He has not forgotten them! The Lord then acknowledges that He recognizes that the people have kept their covenants, despite their trials and difficulties. The people of Alma have been faithful, and whenever women or men of God are faithful in keeping their covenants, they can expect the Lord to keep His promises. ("Remember, the Lord loves effort!"[19])

The Savior then reveals to Alma and his people exactly how He will keep His promise by "deliver[ing] them out of bondage." However, before the Lord delivers them, He assures Alma's people,

> And I will also ease the burdens which are put upon your shoulders, that even you cannot feel them upon your backs, even while you are in bondage; and this will I do that ye may stand as witnesses for me hereafter and that ye may know of a surety that I, the Lord God, do visit my people in their afflictions. And now it came to pass that the burdens which were laid upon Alma and his brethren were made light; yea, the Lord did strengthen them that they could bear up their burdens with ease, and they did submit cheerfully and with patience to all the will of the Lord.[20]

I have always found it interesting that the Lord promises to ease the burdens on their shoulders but does not take their burdens away immediately. If the Lord planned on delivering Alma's people, why wait?

I believe the answer is two-fold. First, the Lord promises to lighten their burdens as a testimony to the people that He is aware of each of them personally ("that ye may know of a surety that I, the Lord God, do visit my people in their afflictions"). It is critical that the people of Alma gain a testimony for themselves that the Lord knows how to perfectly succor each of them in the midst of their hardest trials. He is building their trust in a loving Savior.

The second answer is found in the phrase "yea, the Lord did strengthen them that they could bear up their burdens with ease." The Lord, in His goodness, further blesses Alma and his people by giving them more strength to endure. Gaining greater strength was especially important because after Alma's people escaped bondage, they had further trials ahead that required an even greater fortitude.

The Lord allowed them to continue to carry their burdens but lightened them. Lightening their burdens but not removing them allowed Alma's people to build more "spiritual muscle" to bear future trials with increased faith, patience, and trust. After a season, the Lord delivered them. "And it came to pass that so great was their faith and their patience that the voice of the Lord came unto them again, saying: Be of good comfort, for on the morrow I will deliver you out of bondage."[21]

He strengthened and succored the people of Alma in the midst of their trials. Then, when they had increased in faith and patience, He rescued them all while preparing them for future trials. The Savior's timing was perfect! We worship a God of miracles—a God who does not simply say He will do something, but a loving God that provides every needful thing along the way. We worship a God who is invested in us becoming the very best versions of ourselves.

Sometimes, to become acquainted with our Father in Heaven—to come to really know Him—we must suffer so that when life is unfair, as it will be, we know to whom we can turn. We know who will give us relief and aid, who can truly succor us in our hour of need. We know whom we can trust.

David A. Bednar reassures us:

There is no physical pain, no spiritual wound, no anguish of soul or heartache, no infirmity or weakness you or I ever confront in mortality that the Savior did not experience first. In a moment of weakness, we may cry out, "No one knows what it is like. No one understands." But the Son of God perfectly knows and understands, for He has felt and borne our individual burdens. And because of His infinite and eternal sacrifice (see Alma 34:14), He has perfect empathy and can extend to us His arm of mercy. He can reach out, touch, succor, heal, and strengthen us to be more than we could ever be and help us to do that which we could never do relying only upon our own power. Indeed, His yoke is easy, and His burden is light.[22]

Healed and Whole

C. S. Lewis explains:

> At first, perhaps you understand what He is doing. He is getting the drains right and stopping the leaks in the roof and so on; you knew those jobs needed doing, so you are not surprised. But presently, He starts knocking the house about in a way that hurts abominably and does not seem to make sense. What on earth is He up to? The explanation is He is building quite a different house from the one you thought of, throwing out a new wing here, putting in an extra floor there, running up towers, making courtyards. You thought you were going to be made into a decent little cottage, but He is building a palace.[23]

My divorce was not something that I planned for or even desired, but it happened nonetheless. I learned through the process that I had my own metaphorical "closets to be cleaned, roof to be fixed, and windows to be replaced." What I was not prepared for was the magnitude of change the Lord had in store for me. He lovingly dug up all my old foundations. He strengthened and enlarged my capacity. He patiently taught me to lean unto Him and to trust implicitly in Him.

I discovered "wholeness" did not mean never feeling hurt or sorrow over my divorce. Rather, true healing and wholeness came through allowing the Atonement of Jesus Christ to work in my life daily, over and over again. Healing, then, came as a result of partaking of the precious gift of the Savior's sacrifice on a personal level each day. Healing required turning to the Lord and accepting His will instead of mine. Healing became moving forward day by day with a perfect brightness of hope, trusting the Lord would help me to progress, change, and grow.

Wholeness encompassed accepting responsibility for my part in the story and viewing it through the eyes of a loving and forgiving Savior. Wholeness was a sure knowledge that I had done all I could to right wrongs and move forward into a place of peace and love. Healing meant keeping my covenants and seeking to feel the peace only the Savior can offer. Healing also involved moments of godly sorrow when I recognized old attitudes, fears, thoughts, and ideas.

When these old attitudes or ideas returned to my mind, I willingly laid them at the feet of the Savior. I gave Him all my burdens and turned to Him in all my sorrows. The gift of healing meant that I did not have to let my past define, destroy, or defeat me. Instead, through the enabling power and grace of Christ's Atonement, all things could work together for my good. Through grace, I increased my confidence in a loving Father in Heaven who has a plan for me and knows me by name.

My divorce has taught me to live life deeper, experiencing wholeness and healing from the inside and out. What does a life "living deeper" look like, you ask? For me, it is in the small and simple things. I *focus* on my Savior more than myself. I *trust* my Father in Heaven even when I don't have all the answers, and I *believe* in His timing, the answers will come. I am a better friend, sister, daughter, and mother.

My relationships are richer and more fulfilling. I concentrate on helping each person in my sphere of influence feel the love of the Savior through me. I *know* that everything I experience in this life—including the bad and ugly or the hard and heartbreaking—can and will work together for my good.

How does all the hard and heartbreaking work for my good?

The Lord has promised, "Therefore, he giveth this promise unto you, with an immutable covenant that they shall be fulfilled; and all things wherewith you have been afflicted, shall work together for your good, and to my name's glory, saith the Lord."[24]

The word *immutable* is defined as "changeless." This means that as I keep my covenants, no matter what, the Lord promises that my trials, heartaches, sorrows—all of it—will have a purpose. My trials will not be in vain. I do not have to live daily with endless sorrow and heartache. I can receive healing and grace through the Atonement of Jesus Christ immediately.

As I have come to understand the precious gift of healing more fully, I read the story concerning the woman with an issue of blood, with new understanding.

> And a woman having an issue of blood twelve years, which had spent all her living upon physicians, neither could be healed of any, came behind him, and touched the border of his garment: and immediately her issue of blood staunched. And Jesus said, who touched me? When all denied, Peter and they that were with him said, Master, the multitude throng thee and press thee, and sayest thou, Who touched me? And Jesus said somebody hath touched me: for I perceive that virtue is gone out of me. And when the woman saw that she was not hid, she came trembling and falling down before him, she declared unto him before all the people for what cause she had touched him, and how she was healed immediately. And he said unto her, Daughter, be of good comfort: thy faith hath made thee whole; go in peace.[25]

This woman lived for years with the pain and sorrow of not being able to bear children. She was considered unclean by members of her faith and was an outsider, a pariah to society. She futilely spent all she owned, trying to find a cure. She learned about the Savior, and in her desperation for healing, she believed if she could touch even the smallest part of the Savior's clothing, she would be healed.

Her opportunity to see the Savior came through a crowd of people. She reached forward and in total faith grasped the hem of His garment. In that instant, her faith was rewarded—she was fully healed. This was truly a life-changing miracle!

Through the Savior's grace, she was able to touch the hem of His robe and be healed. She no longer had to wait to be made whole. Her healing was instantaneous because of the divine power of the Lord's Atonement. And because of her faith, coupled with the Savior's grace, she was assured, "Be of good comfort, *thy* faith hath made thee whole."

It is important to note that we meet the woman with the issue of blood at the moment of her healing—the peak of her miracle. We do not know the depths of this woman's sorrow, how many years she suffered, how many seemingly unanswered prayers she uttered, or how long she waited in faith hoping for some kind of miracle.

We are given only a glimpse at the end of a very long chapter in the woman's life and a peek into the beginning of a new chapter for her. Elder Carpenter reminds us:

> Jesus Christ can heal more than just our physical bodies. He can heal our spirits as well. Throughout scripture, we learn how Christ helped those whose spirits were weak and made them whole. As we ponder these experiences, our hope, and faith in the Savior's power to bless our lives increases. Jesus Christ can change our hearts, heal us from the effects of injustice or abuse we may experience, and strengthen our capacity to bear loss and heartache, bringing us peace to help us endure the trials of our lives, healing us emotionally [and physically.][26]

Healing comes only through the Atonement of Jesus Christ and is a promise of covenant living. Complete healing might not come in this life, but it is a promise that is ours to claim as we continue to keep our covenants. Remember, "I, the Lord, am bound when ye do what I say."[27] He is bound to us, as we live our covenants.

Through righteous covenant-belonging, we are guaranteed every blessing. This is a sure promise. President Nelson words affirm this truth: "Your commitment to follow the Savior by making covenants with Him and then keeping those covenants will open the door to every spiritual blessing and privilege available to men, women, and children everywhere."[28]

My divorce allowed the Lord to restore my soul, heal it, and make it whole through my Savior. However, my healing did not mean that my life went back together, as if my divorce had never happened. Nor did it mean that I never felt heartache and sorrow over the past. Healing through the Savior's Atonement allowed my past to serve a purpose.

The woman who touched the Savior's hem also discovered this truth—her life did not return to what it had been. Her healing did not change her past, but her past now stood as a testament—a testament to the endless power and mercy of our Savior Jesus Christ and His ability to heal us wholly, completely, and perfectly. Elder Holland promises, "Through the great miracle of the Atonement of Jesus Christ, He will give your heart back to you healed and whole."[29]

What did the woman's life look like after she was healed and made whole? What does anyone's life look like after becoming acquainted with the Savior and experiencing firsthand His healing power?

Unfortunately, we have only one line of scripture to give us an inkling of what perhaps came next for this woman: "She declared unto him before all the people for what cause she had touched him and how she was healed immediately."[30]

She boldly declared to the crowd of onlookers her very personal reason for touching the Savior's hem and the miraculous outcome of being fully healed. I can imagine her joyful return to her family, friends, and even her physicians. She could not wait to share the miracle of healing she had received. She would never forget that moment! Her single act of faith forever changed her life.

Jairus is another person who encountered the Lord in his lifetime. He had a daughter who became sick and then died. This father could not accept that this was the end of his beloved child, and he sought out the healing power of the Savior. Others mocked and scorned Jairus—claiming his hopes were in vain. The Savior responded, "Fear not: believe only, and she shall be made whole."[31] Then, Jesus Christ made her whole!

Consider the promise found in Lord's words he said to Jairus: "Fear not: believe only, and she shall be made whole." His words give encouragement and point to the promise for each of us. Do not fear, only believe, and trust that *you*, too, can be made whole.

All who encountered the Savior were changed forever by His presence. The twelve apostles who tarried with the Lord were privileged to know and understand the divinity of the Master they followed. These twelve men had special calling to share their knowledge of the beloved Jesus Christ all the rest of their days.

They wrote down His miracles. They taught them to others. They baptized in His name. They brought many to the truth of the gospel. They spent their days in service to the Lord until every breath, every task, every part of their lives had been performed with praise and thanksgiving to the Savior for His matchless gift.

This is my intention, as well.

Love and grace
Brought him here
A world to save
He suffered all
He felt our pain
He knew it was the only way

He understands
When I'm unsure
He knows the plan
And when I'm tired
Losing my way
He picks me up and gives me strength
And I will praise Him

All my days
All my days
May my voice ring out in praise

For him who died
To give me life
I will glory in His name
All my days

He sends his love
So patiently
He teaches me
Step by Step
Leading me home
It's the greatest love I've ever known
And I will praise Him

And when I see Him again
I will bow down and say
All my days, all my days,
May my voice ring out in praise,
For him who died to give me life,
I will glory in His name.
All my days.[32] (Hilary Weeks)

The words penned in this song echo how I feel after my divorce. I have a life—a life more fully dedicated to God, a life spent breathing in and breathing out my praise and testimony of the healing and atoning blood of my Savior, Jesus Christ. Until all my minutes, all my hours, and all my days are spent in service to and in gratitude of the Lord. He is the one who has comforted me. He is the one who has healed me. He is the one that has confirmed to me: "Thy faith hath made thee whole. Go in peace."[33]

He has made of my ashes—beauty.

Works Cited

Introduction

1. Renlund, Dale G. "Latter-day Saints Keep on Trying." General Conference, The Church of Jesus Christ of Latter-day Saints, April 2015, Salt Lake City, Utah.

Prologue

1. Uchtdorf, Dieter F. "Your Happily Ever After." General Conference, The Church of Jesus Christ of Latter-day Saints, April 2010, Salt Lake City, Utah.

Chapter 1: The Beginning

1. Holland, Jeffrey R. "Lessons from Liberty Jail." Brigham Young University devotional, 7 September 2008.
2. Hinckley, Gordon B. "Watch the Switches in your Life." General Conference, The Church of Jesus Christ of Latter-day Saints, January 1973, Salt Lake City, Utah.
3. Brown, Leon, quoted by Robert Tew. "You Must Take Responsibility for Your Own." *Live Life Happy*, 6 July 2014, www.livelifehappy.com/life-quotes/you-must-take-responsibility-for-your-own/. Accessed 9 October 2020.
4. Cloud, Henry and John Sims Townsend. *Boundaries.* Zondervan, 1992, 27–28.
5. Uchtdorf, Dieter F. "Fourth Floor, Last Door." General Conference, The Church of Jesus Christ of Latter-day Saints, October 2016, Salt Lake City, Utah.
6. Dew, Sheri. "Sheri Dew: How to Open the Heavens and Hear the Answers the Spirit Is Speaking to You." *LDS Living*, 13 May 2017, www.ldsliving.com/Sheri-Dew-How-to-Open-the-Heavens-and-Hear-the-Answers-the-Spirit-Is-Speaking-to-You/s/85347. Accessed 9 October 2020.
7. Day, Laurel C. "One Heart, One Mind." Time Out for Women, Deseret Book, July 2016.
8. Jacob 5:47.
9. Andersen, Neil L. "Wounded." General Conference, The Church of Jesus Christ of Latter-day Saints, October 2018, Salt Lake City, Utah.

10. Cox, Paul Alan. "An Eternal Perspective." Brigham Young University devotional, 10 October 1995.
11. Mormon 5:23.
12. Monson, Thomas S. "Be of Good Cheer." General Conference, The Church of Jesus Christ of Latter-day Saints, April 2009, Salt Lake City, Utah.
13. Moroni 10:4–5.

Chapter 2: Joy Amid Sorrow

1. Monson, Thomas S. "The Spirit Giveth Life." General Conference, The Church of Jesus Christ of Latter-day Saints, April 1985, Salt Lake City, Utah.
2. Aburto, Reyna I. "With One Accord." General Conference, The Church of Jesus Christ of Latter-day Saints, April 2018, Salt Lake City, Utah.
3. Dew, Sheri, quoted by Carrian Cheney. "Fighting for Faith in the Darkness Part 15." *Oh Sweet Basil*, 25 July 2019, www.ohsweetbasil.com/fighting-for-faith-in-the-darkness-part-15/. Accessed 10 October 2020.
4. Eyring, Henry B. "The Caregiver." General Conference, The Church of Jesus Christ of Latter-day Saints, October 2012, Salt Lake City, Utah.
5. Esplin, Cheryl A. "He Asks us to be His Hands." General Conference, The Church of Jesus Christ of Latter-day Saints, April 2016, Salt Lake City, Utah.
6. Kimball, Spencer W. "Small Acts of Service," *Ensign*, December 1974.
7. "Sealing Policies." *General Handbook: Serving in The Church of Jesus Christ of Latter-day Saints.* The Church of Jesus Christ of Latter-day Saints, January 2020, section 38.5.
8. Bednar, David A. "The Tender Mercies of the Lord." General Conference, The Church of Jesus Christ of Latter-day Saints, April 2005, Salt Lake City, Utah.
9. Uchtdorf, Dieter F. "You Matter to Him." General Conference, The Church of Jesus Christ of Latter-day Saints, October 2011, Salt Lake City, Utah.
10. "May God bless the woman deep within me, the woman I'm trying to be . . . ." *Orthodox Christianity*, 13 July 2018, www.orthodoxchristianity.info/may-god-bless-the-woman-deep-within-me-the-woman-im-trying-to-be/. Accessed 10 October 2020.
11. Nelson, Russell M. "Drawing the Power of Jesus Christ into our Lives." General Conference, The Church of Jesus Christ of Latter-day Saints, April 2017, Salt Lake City, Utah.
12. Renlund, Dale G. "Consider the Goodness and Greatness of God." General Conference, The Church of Jesus Christ of Latter-day Saints, April 2020, Salt Lake City, Utah.
13. Luke 5:31.
14. 3 Nephi 17:7.
15. Matthew 9:35.
16. Alma 7:11–12.

17. 3 Nephi 25:2.
18. Colossians 2:2.
19. Mosiah 18:21.
20. Ezekiel 36:26.
21. 3 Nephi 12:8.
22. Hinckley, Gordon B. "Put your Trust in God," *Ensign*, February 2006.
23. Nelson, Russell M. "Men's Hearts Shall Fail Them." *YouTube,* uploaded by The Church of Jesus Christ of Latter-day Saints, 18 November 2011, www.youtu.be/EMwKxmTLaCs. Accessed 10 October 2020.

Chapter 3: Foundation in Christ

1. Scott, Richard G. "The Transforming Power of Faith and Character." General Conference, The Church of Jesus Christ of Latter-day Saints, October 2010, Salt Lake City, Utah.
2. 3 Nephi 14:24–27.
3. Helaman 5:12.
4. Luke 10:38–42.
5. Uchtdorf, Dieter F. "Of Things that Matter Most." General Conference, The Church of Jesus Christ of Latter-day Saints, October 2010, Salt Lake City, Utah.
6. Holland, Jeffrey R. "This, the Greatest of All Dispensations," *Ensign*, July 2007.
7. Holland, Patricia T. "One Thing Needful: Becoming Women of Greater Faith in Christ," *Ensign*, October 1987.
8. Uchtdorf, Dieter F. "Happiness, Our Heritage." General Conference, The Church of Jesus Christ of Latter-day Saints, October 2008, Salt Lake City, Utah.
9. 2 Nephi 15:25; emphasis added.
10. 2 Nephi 19:12, 21; emphasis added.
11. Ballard, M. Russell. "25 LDS Quotes to Tape to Your Mirror Immediately." *LDS Living*, 1 June 2017, www.ldsliving.com/25-LDS-Quotes-to-Tape-to-Your-Mirror-Immediately/s/85509. Accessed 11 October 2020.
12. Ballard, M. Russell. "Men and Women and Priesthood Power," *Ensign*, September 2014.
13. Nelson, Wendy Watson. " . . . My soul delighteth in the covenants of the Lord." Brigham Young University Women's Conference, 30 April 2015.
14. Monson, Thomas S. "Blessings of the Temple," *Ensign*, October 2010.
15. 1 Nephi 8:12, 15.
16. Alma 17:9, 11.
17. Ether 12:27.
18. Oaks, Dallin H. "The Challenge to Become," *Ensign*, October 2000

Chapter 4: Healing and Forgiveness

1. Ashton, Marvin J. "If Thou Endure It Well." General Conference, The Church of Jesus Christ of Latter-day Saints, October 1984, Salt Lake City, Utah.
2. Hales, Robert D. "Waiting Upon the Lord: Thy Will be Done." General Conference, The Church of Jesus Christ of Latter-day Saints, October 2011, Salt Lake City, Utah.
3. Holland, Jeffrey R. "'Remember Lot's Wife': Faith Is for the Future." Brigham Young University Devotional, 13 January 2009.
4. Bednar, David A. "Accepting the Lord's Will and Timing," *Ensign*, August 2016.
5. Doctrine and Covenants 64:7, 9.
6. Doctrine and Covenants 64:10.
7. Ten Boom, Corrie. *The Hiding Place*. Bantam Books, 1971.
8. Ibid.
9. Holland, Jeffrey R. "The Ministry of Reconciliation." General Conference, The Church of Jesus Christ of Latter-day Saints, October 2018, Salt Lake City, Utah.
10. Anderson, Neil T. *goodreads*, www.goodreads.com/quotes/463435-don-t-wait-to-forgive-until-you-feel-like-forgiving-you. Accessed 11 October 2020.
11. Holland, Jeffrey R. "The Ministry of Reconciliation." General Conference, The Church of Jesus Christ of Latter-day Saints, October 2018, Salt Lake City, Utah.
12. Uchtdorf, Dieter F. "Point of Safe Return." General Conference, The Church of Jesus Christ of Latter-day Saints, April 2007, Salt Lake City, Utah.
13. Clark, Kim B. "Look unto Jesus Christ." General Conference, The Church of Jesus Christ of Latter-day Saints, April 2019, Salt Lake City, Utah.
14. 3 Nephi 10:4.
15. Renlund, Dale G. "Latter-day Saints Keep on Trying." General Conference, The Church of Jesus Christ of Latter-day Saints, April 2015, Salt Lake City, Utah.
16. Wirthlin, Joseph B. "Finding a Safe Harbor." General Conference, The Church of Jesus Christ of Latter-day Saints, April 2000, Salt Lake City, Utah.
17. Hinckley, Gordon B. "Forgiveness." General Conference, The Church of Jesus Christ of Latter-day Saints, October 2005, Salt Lake City, Utah.

Chapter 5: Forgiveness and Boundaries

1. Eyring, Henry B. "That We May Be One." General Conference, The Church of Jesus Christ of Latter-day Saints, April 1998, Salt Lake City, Utah.
2. Cloud, Henry and John Sims Townsend. *Boundaries*. Zondervan, 1992, 45–46.
3. Alma 30:29.

4. Echo Hawk, Larry J. "Even as Christ Forgives You, So Also Do Ye." General Conference, The Church of Jesus Christ of Latter-day Saints, April 2018, Salt Lake City, Utah.
5. Uchtdorf, Dieter F. "The Reflection in the Water." Church Educational System Fireside, The Church of Jesus Christ of Latter-day Saints, 1 November 2009, Provo, Utah.
6. Uchtdorf, Dieter F. "The Merciful Obtain Mercy." General Conference, The Church of Jesus Christ of Latter-day Saints, April 2012, Salt Lake City, Utah.
7. Ether 10:28.
8. Alma 2:28.
9. Alma 30:58–60.
10. Benson, Ezra Taft. "A Message to the Rising Generation." General Conference, The Church of Jesus Christ of Latter-day Saints, October 1977, Salt Lake City, Utah.
11. Matthew 18:21–22.
12. Doctrine and Covenants 98:39–48.
13. Doctrine and Covenants 82:10.
14. Uchtdorf, Dieter F. "The Merciful Obtain Mercy." General Conference, The Church of Jesus Christ of Latter-day Saints, April 2012, Salt Lake City, Utah.
15. Shakespeare, William. *King Lear.* Ed. Tom Smith. Oxford: Globe Theater Press, 2005.
16. Doctrine and Covenants 58:42.
17. Oaks, Dallin H. "Judge Not and Judging." Brigham Young University Devotional, 1 March 1998.
18. Griffin, Tyler J. "How Do We 'Judge Righteous Judgment'?" *Ensign*, February 2019.
19. Moroni 7:16.
20. Uchtdorf, Dieter F. "The Merciful Obtain Mercy." General Conference, The Church of Jesus Christ of Latter-day Saints, April 2012, Salt Lake City, Utah.
21. Eyring, Henry B. "Where is the Pavilion?" General Conference, The Church of Jesus Christ of Latter-day Saints, October 2012.

Chapter 6: Steadfast and Immovable

1. Andersen, Neil L. "Trial of Your Faith." General Conference, The Church of Jesus Christ of Latter-day Saints, October 2012, Salt Lake City, Utah.
2. Johnson, Peter M. "Power to Overcome the Adversary." General Conference, The Church of Jesus Christ of Latter-day Saints, October 2019, Salt Lake City, Utah.
3. 2 Nephi 26:22.
4. Brontë, Charlotte. *Jane Eyre.* 3rd Ed., Bantam Books, 1981, pp. 342–43.
5. Nelson, Wendy Watson. "'. . .My soul delighteth in the covenants of the Lord.'" Brigham Young University Women's Conference, 30 April 2015.

6. Smith, Eldred G. "Choose Ye This Day." Conference Report, The Church of Jesus Christ of Latter-day Saints, April 1970.
7. Maxwell, Neal A. "'Swallowed Up In the Will of the Father.'" General Conference, The Church of Jesus Christ of Latter-day Saints, October 1995, Salt Lake City, Utah.
8. Scott, Richard G. "Make the Exercise of Faith your First Priority." General Conference, The Church of Jesus Christ of Latter-day Saints, November 2014, Salt Lake City, Utah.
9. Christofferson, D. Todd. "The Divine Gift of Repentance." General Conference, The Church of Jesus Christ of Latter-day Saints, October 2011, Salt Lake City, Utah.
10. Nelson, Russell M. "We Can Do Better and Be Better." General Conference, The Church of Jesus Christ of Latter-day Saints, April 2019, Salt Lake City, Utah.
11. Alma 36:18–20.
12. Worthen, Kevin J. "Enduring Joy." Brigham Young University Devotional, 7 January 2020, Provo, Utah.
13. Smith, Joseph, quoted by James E. Faust. "Our Search for Happiness," *Ensign*, October 2000.
14. 2 Nephi 2:25.
15. Worthen, ibid.
16. Rasband, Ronald A. "Let the Holy Spirit Guide." General Conference, The Church of Jesus Christ of Latter-day Saints, April 2017, Salt Lake City, Utah.
17. 2 Corinthians 5:7.
18. Murdock, Eric B. "Tune In to the Spirit." *New Era*, The Church of Jesus Christ of Latter-day Saints, June 2014. www.churchofjesuschrist.org/study/new-era/2014/06/tune-in-to-the-spirit?lang=eng. Accessed 14 October 2020.
19. Faust, James E. "Voice of the Spirit." General Conference, The Church of Jesus Christ of Latter-day Saints, June 2006, Salt Lake City, Utah.
20. Nelson, Russell M. "Revelation for the Church, Revelation for our Lives." General Conference, The Church of Jesus Christ of Latter-day Saints, April 2018, Salt Lake City, Utah.
21. Ibid.
22. Matthew 7:13–14.
23. Alma 38:9.
24. Uchtdorf, Dieter F. "Your Great Adventure." General Conference, The Church of Jesus Christ of Latter-day Saints, October 2019, Salt Lake City, Utah.
25. 3 Nephi 6:14.

Chapter 7: Partnering with Jesus Christ

1. Burton, Linda K. "Certain Women." General Conference, The Church of Jesus Christ of Latter-day Saints, April 2017, Salt Lake City, Utah.

2. Beck, Julie B. "'And Upon the Handmaids in Those Days Will I Pour Out My Spirit.'" General Conference, The Church of Jesus Christ of Latter-day Saints, April 2010, Salt Lake City, Utah.
3. Nelson, Russell M. "Revelation for the Church, Revelation for our Lives." General Conference, The Church of Jesus Christ of Latter-day Saints, April 2018, Salt Lake City, Utah.
4. Beck, Julie B. "'And Upon the Handmaids in Those Days Will I Pour Out My Spirit.'" General Conference, The Church of Jesus Christ of Latter-day Saints, April 2010, Salt Lake City, Utah.
5. 2 Timothy 1:7.
6. Holland, Matthew. "Wrong Roads and Revelation." *New Era*, The Church of Jesus Christ of Latter-day Saints, July 2005.
7. Bingham, Jean B., Sharon Eubank, and Reyna I. Aburto. "'Endowed with Priesthood Power.'" Brigham Young University Women's Conference, 2 May 2019, Provo, Utah.
8. Alma 37:17.
9. Nelson, Russell M. "Revelation for the Church, Revelation for our Lives." General Conference, The Church of Jesus Christ of Latter-day Saints, April 2018, Salt Lake City, Utah.
10. Gong, Gerrit W. "Covenant Belonging." General Conference, The Church of Jesus Christ of Latter-day Saints, October 2019, Salt Lake City, Utah.
11. Burton, Linda K. "The Power, Joy, and Love of Covenant Keeping." General Conference, The Church of Jesus Christ of Latter-day Saints, October 2013, Salt Lake City, Utah.
12. 1 Nephi 2:16, 19–20.
13. 1 Nephi 3:7.
14. 1 Nephi 4:6.
15. 1 Nephi 17:1–2.
16. Smith, Joseph, quoted in "Sacrifice." *Guide to the Scriptures, The Church of Jesus Christ of Latter-day Saints*, www.churchofjesuschrist.org/study/scriptures/gs/sacrifice?lang=eng. Accessed 17 October 2020.
17. 2 Nephi 5:27.
18. Renlund, Dale G. "Abound with Blessings." General Conference, The Church of Jesus Christ of Latter-day Saints, April 2019, Salt Lake City, Utah.
19. Hebrews 11:13.
20. Nelson, Russell M., quoted by R. Scott Lloyd. "Elder Nelson Delivers Spiritual Thanksgiving Feast to MTCs." *Church News*, 4 December 2013, www.churchofjesuschrist.org/church/news/elder-nelson-delivers-spiritual-thanksgiving-feast-to-mtcs?lang=eng. Accessed 17 October 2020.
21. Renlund, Dale G. "Abound with Blessings." General Conference, The Church of Jesus Christ of Latter-day Saints, April 2019, Salt Lake City, Utah.
22. Romans 8:28.
23. Alma 57:21.

24. Nelson, Russell M. "The Love and Laws of God." Brigham Young University Devotional, 17 September 2019, Provo, Utah.
25. 1 Nephi 4:1.
26. Faust, James E. "President Faust counsels: Have positive attitude in missionary work." *Church News*, 25 June 1999, www.thechurchnews.com/archives/1999-06-26/president-faust-counsels-have-positive-attitude-in-missionary-work-123092. Accessed 17 October 2020.
27. Hinckley, Marjorie Pay, quoted by Linda K. Burton. "Priesthood Power—Available to All," *Ensign*, June 2014

Chapter 8: Thy Faith Hath Made Thee Whole

1. Holland, Jeffrey R. "Lessons from Liberty Jail." Brigham Young University Devotional, 7 September 2008, Provo, Utah.
2. Quoted in Pugmire, Genelle. "1898–2010: Provo Tabernacle remembered as gathering place." *Daily Herald*, 18 December 2010, www.heraldextra.com/news/local/1898-2010-provo-tabernacle-remembered-as-gathering-place/article_f78997a6-0a3b-11e0-abe0-001cc4c002e0.html. Accessed 17 October 2020.
3. Curtis, John, quoted by Caleb Warnock. "Provo announces community gathering, concert for tabernacle," *Daily Herald*, 18 December 2010, www.heraldextra.com/tabernacle/article_6bdbb3a6-30a3-5264-be06-134e88e9ae1b.html. Accessed 17 October 2020.
4. Curtis, John, quoted by Cassidy Hansen. "From tabernacle to temple: the transformation of Provo's timeless epicenter." Provo, Utah: *The Daily Universe*, 11 January 2016, www.universe.byu.edu/2016/01/11/from-tabernacle-to-temple-the-transformation-of-provos-timeless-epicenter1/. Accessed 17 October 2020.
5. Monson, Thomas S. "As We Meet Again." General Conference, The Church of Jesus Christ of Latter-day Saints, October 2011, Salt Lake City, Utah.
6. Hales, Robert D. "Faith through Tribulation Brings Peace and Joy." General Conference, The Church of Jesus Christ of Latter-day Saints, April 2003, Salt Lake City, Utah.
7. Cook, Quentin L. "Foundations of Faith." General Conference, The Church of Jesus Christ of Latter-day Saints, April 2017, Salt Lake City, Utah.
8. 1 Peter 1:7.
9. "The Silversmith—Refiner and Purifier." *Six Notes Clothing*, 13 September 2019, www.sixnotesclothing.com/blog/refinerandpurifier. Accessed 17 October 2020.
10. Matthew 5:48.
11. Isaiah 53:5.
12. Isaiah 53:5.
13. Gabbott, Mabel Jones. "He Sent His Son." *Children's Songbook*. The Church of Jesus Christ of Latter-day Saints, 1989.
14. Eyring, Henry B. "The Comforter." General Conference, The Church of Jesus Christ of Latter-day Saints, April 2015, Salt Lake City, Utah.

15. Matthew 11:28–30.
16. Bednar, David A. "Bear Up their Burdens With Ease." General Conference, The Church of Jesus Christ of Latter-day Saints, April 2014, Salt Lake City, Utah.
17. Mosiah 24:9–12.
18. Mosiah 24:13.
19. Nelson, Russell M., and Joy D. Jones. "An Especially Noble Calling." General Conference, The Church of Jesus Christ of Latter-day Saints, April 2020, Salt Lake City, Utah.
20. Mosiah 24:14–15.
21. Mosiah 24:16.
22. Bednar, David A. "Bear Up their Burdens With Ease." General Conference, The Church of Jesus Christ of Latter-day Saints, April 2014, Salt Lake City, Utah.
23. Lewis, C. S. *Mere Christianity*. New York, Touchstone, 1996, 175–176.
24. Doctrine and Covenants 98:3.
25. Luke 8:43–48.
26. Carpenter, Matthew L. "Wilt Thou Be Made Whole?" General Conference, The Church of Jesus Christ of Latter-day Saints, October 2018, Salt Lake City, Utah.
27. Doctrine and Covenants 82:10.
28. Nelson, Russell M. "As We Go Forward Together," *Ensign*, April 2018
29. Holland, Jeffrey R. *For Times of Trouble: Spiritual Solace from the Psalms*. Salt Lake City, Utah: Deseret Book, 2012.
30. Luke 8:47.
31. Luke 8:50.
32. Weeks, Hilary. "All My Days." *He Hears Me*. Salt Lake City, Utah, Deseret Book, 1996.
33. Luke 8:48.

NOTE: Scriptural quotations are taken from the following versions of the respective books:

The Book of Mormon. Salt Lake City: The Church of Jesus Christ of Latter-day Saints, 2013.

The Holy Bible: Authorized King James Version. Salt Lake: The Church of Jesus Christ of Latter-day Saints, 2013.

The Doctrine and Covenants of The Church of Jesus Christ of Latter-day Saints. Salt Lake City, Utah: The Church of Jesus Christ of Latter-day Saints, 2013.

Acknowledgments

Thank you to my dear family and friends who have supported me throughout this challenging and often emotional endeavor. I could not have written this book without your love and support.

A special thanks to the Duvall Women's Discussion group who willingly read the first extremely rough draft and gave me the encouragement to keep trying.

Thank you also to Megan Neville, a dear friend, who read every single word I wrote, even the worst ones, and gave me loving and constructive feedback every time.

Thank you to Kathryn Thompson for her willingness to share honest opinions, and for all of her hard-earned experiences in the publishing world.

Thank you to Sarah Hale for being an amazing neighbor by letting me borrow various sundry items from her pantry—also for her mad indexing and artistic skills!

A most especial thanks to my editors, Danielle Everton and Dawn Craner. These women worked tirelessly to help me hone my craft and encourage me. They also lovingly told me all the things I did not want to acknowledge but needed to hear. Without their assistance, I would be half the writer.

About the Author

Noelle McBride was born and raised in the Pacific Northwest. After having been blessed with three children during a seventeen-year marriage, she went through a difficult and heartbreaking divorce. Notwithstanding this hardship, Noelle experienced much healing and hope in her personal life through the Atonement of Jesus Christ. Desiring to help other women navigate the same trial, Noelle shares the promises and peace of the gospel in her first published book, *Beauty for Ashes: Divorce and the Latter-day Saint Woman.*

Noelle is a professional motivational speaker and teacher with over twenty years of experience, counseling and teaching women in groups and individually. She currently leads women in gospel-based workshops that are focused on overcoming the trials and hardships of divorce. She also serves as an ordinance worker in the Seattle Washington Temple and in her stake Relief Society presidency. After a season as a single parent, Noelle eventually remarried a widower in the Columbia River Washington Temple. They are now raising all six of their children together and learning the joys of navigating a blended family. On rainy days, you can find Noelle curled up in front of a fire with a warm cup of tea and a good book.